HYSTERIA

A JOURNEY THROUGH HISTORY AND MENTAL HEALTH

DR RANI CHAWLA

GLOBAL EAST-WEST (LONDON)

CONTENTS

CHAPTER ONE

INTRODUCTION TO HYSTERIA: PAST AND PRESENT

Historical Context and Significance

HYSTERIA, AN ENIGMATIC PHENOMENON, finds its roots deeply embedded within the cultural and societal tapestries of diverse historical epochs (Cramer, 2018). Its genesis and metamorphosis are intricately tied to the prevailing ideologies, mores, and attitudes surrounding sexuality, gender paradigms, and mental health. The origins of hysteria can be traced to antiquity, specifically ancient Egypt, where it was postulated through the 'wandering womb' theory—an early manifestation of the patriarchal perspective on femininity and its biological processes (Layne, 2019). The Greco-Roman period further entrenched hysteria as a condition predominantly afflicting women, thereby bolstering societal convictions regarding female emotional fragility and volatility (Micale, 1989). Esteemed philosophers such as Plato and Aristotle lent credence to this viewpoint, perpetuating the belief that a 'defective' reproductive system rendered women particularly susceptible to emotional turmoil.

In medieval Europe, the narrative surrounding hysteria evolved, intertwining with the supernatural; it was often perceived as a consequence of witchcraft or demonic possession (Tasca et al., 2012). This era represented a confluence of religious orthodoxy and medical superstitions, casting a shadow over those, particularly women, who exhibited symptoms of hysteria. The Renaissance transformed the medical discourses surrounding hysteria, albeit still constrained by prevailing moral frameworks and ethical considerations (Showalter, 2018).

The 19th century heralded pivotal shifts in the comprehension and treatment of hysteria, distinctly articulated through the seminal contributions of figures like Jean-Martin Charcot and Sigmund Freud. Charcot's groundbreaking clinical investigations at the Salpêtrière in Paris laid the foundational stones for contemporary neurology (Carveth & Carveth, 2004), while Freud's psychoanalytic theories unveiled novel insights into the psychological substrata of hysteria (Paster, 2017). These advancements unfolded against the backdrop of broader societal upheavals, notably the burgeoning women's rights movement and a gradual evolution in the attitudes toward mental illness (Bustos et al., 2014).

The historical import of hysteria transcends its medical and psychological dimensions, serving as a mirror reflecting pervasive gender dynamics, cultural anxieties, and the ever-evolving nexus between science, religion, and society (Illis, 2002).

Defining Hysteria: A Complex Medical Term

The designation 'hysteria' emerges as a contentious and evolving term within the annals of medical history (Micale, 1996). Its implications have morphed across epochs, mirroring societal attitudes towards emotional and psychological distress. Deriving from its etymological roots in ancient Greek, where it was closely tied to the uterus, hysteria's modern complexities within psychiatry present an enigma that continues to bewitch medical practitioners and scholars alike (Cramer, 2018).

To fathom the intricacies of hysteria demands a thorough exploration of its conceptual evolution through the ages, as the term has historically functioned as a catch-all diagnosis for many inexplicable symptoms and behaviors. Initially confined to women, it was linked to the notion of a nomadic uterus causing physical and mental ailments, yet it eventually expanded to incorporate a spectrum of obscure neurotic symptoms affecting both genders (Bailey, 1966). This transformation paints a vivid portrait of the shifting attitudes toward mental health and psychosomatic disorders through time (Layne, 2019).

Moreover, the medicalization of hysteria incited fervent debates regarding its conceptualization and categorization within psychiatric practice. As we delve deeper into both historical and contemporary interpretations of hysteria, it becomes manifest that its definition is layered with medical intricacies and cultural underpinnings (Cramer, 2018). The intertwining of gender, power dynamics, and societal expectations has profoundly impacted how individuals branded as 'hysterical' are perceived and depicted (Paster, 2017). Unraveling this multifaceted term necessitates critically examining the interplay between medical knowledge, sociocultural constructs, and personal experiences.

Given the convoluted nature of defining hysteria, it is paramount to recognize the limitations inherent in historical interpretations, all while aspiring to uncover a more nuanced comprehension of the term. By deconstructing the myriad layers of meaning associated with hysteria, we can glean insights into broader matters relating to the stigmatization of mental health and representations of psychological distress (Carveth & Carveth, 2004). As we embark upon this intellectual odyssey, a sensitive and open-minded approach is essential to navigate the intricate tapestry of perspectives surrounding this complex medical designation (Paster, 2017).

Review of Early Documentation and Reports

The scholarly inquiry into hysteria unfolds as an exploration of historical records illuminating the evolution of medical comprehension and societal perceptions of this intricate condition. Scrutinizing early documentation and reports affords us the opportunity to trace the genesis of hysteria back to ancient civilizations, spanning from the Egyptians' papyrus manuscripts to the accounts chronicled within Greek and Roman medical treatises (Micale, 1989). These texts provide invaluable insights into how this elusive disorder was conceptualized across cultures and eras, thereby establishing its enduring influence on medical discourse throughout history.

Upon surveying the earliest references to hysteria, we encounter a rich tapestry of descriptions that offer diverse perspectives and interpretations (Bustos et al., 2014). Beyond the confines of strictly medical literature, we must also engage with literary, philosophical, and religious texts to appreciate the holistic ramifications of hysteria on human experience and belief systems (Layne, 2019). The ubiquity of these narratives underscores the profound impact this disorder has wielded over the collective consciousness of societies through time.

One notable aspect of early documentation is the persistent motif of the 'wandering womb,' a concept that infiltrates ancient medical literature and suggests the prevailing theories concerning the etiology of hysteria in women (Tasca et al., 2012). This notion, attributing a peripatetic uterus as the source of various somatic and emotional disturbances, reflects the entrenched gender biases prevalent in early medical understanding. By investigating these initial reports, we enhance our understanding of how cultural and social beliefs pervade the perception and treatment of hysteria (Carveth & Carveth, 2004).

In our examination of early documentation, the pioneering contributions of significant historical figures in the understanding of hysteria cannot be overlooked. From Hippocrates to Galen, their influential writings delineate symptoms and propose treatments that lay the groundwork for future medical discourse on this fascinating malady (Micale, 1989). Additionally, the voices of lesser-known female contemporaries, whose insights and interpretations of hysteria often remain eclipsed by their male counterparts, merit appreciation and acknowledgment (Showalter, 2018).

This exploration of early documentation and reports offers a comprehensive vista of the intricate weave fashioned by centuries of observations and interpretations of hysteria. It serves as a pivotal foundation for grasping the complexities inherent in our contemporary understanding of this condition, setting the stage for an exhaustive investigation of the evolving theories and philosophies that have shaped modern perspectives on this enigmatic disorder (Bustos et al., 2014).

Evolving Theories and Philosophies

The comprehension of hysteria throughout history has been indelibly shaped by an array of evolving theories and philosophies. This multifaceted medical phenomenon has been subject to diverse interpretations, spanning from the archaic notion of the 'wandering womb' to the modern psychological paradigms articulated by notable medical luminaries (Cramer, 2018). A thorough investigation into these evolving theories and philosophies is essential to grasp the depth of historical perspectives on hysteria.

Early theories surrounding hysteria often mirrored the societal attitudes prevalent concerning women's health and comportment. From Hippocrates' conceptualization of the errant womb to Galen's humoral theory, these ancient beliefs provided the scaffold for subsequent medical discourse surrounding hysteria (Illis,

2002). Moreover, the inseparable links between mental and physical health shaped the treatment methodologies directed at those deemed afflicted by hysteria (Bustos et al., 2014).

The Renaissance represented a significant philosophical pivot in the conceptualization of hysteria. During this epoch, the nascent embrace of scientific reasoning and empirical scrutiny intermingled with superstition and doctrinaire beliefs (Layne, 2019). Practitioners such as Paracelsus contributed to the emergence of eclectic medical theories, merging alchemical traditions with established medical knowledge (Carveth & Carveth, 2004). This period was also marked by an intensified focus on individual case studies, allowing for meticulous documentation of the symptoms and treatments associated with hysteria.

The 19th century heralded a paradigmatic shift in the medical theories related to hysteria, particularly with the emergence of transformative figures like Jean-Martin Charcot and Sigmund Freud. Charcot's pioneering endeavors in neurology and hypnosis elucidated hysteria as a neurological disorder, dismantling earlier misconceptions (Cramer, 2018). Concurrently, Freud's psychoanalytic theories proposed that hysteria was rooted in repressed psychological conflicts, fundamentally altering the landscape of mental health and laying the groundwork for contemporary psychotherapy (Paster, 2017).

Additionally, the confluence of gender, psychology, and medicine played a crucial role in molding the evolving theories and philosophies concerning hysteria. The patriarchal lens through which hysteria was scrutinized perpetuated myths and stigmas, leading to the pathologization of feminine emotions and experiences (Showalter, 2018). As societal perspectives advanced, so too did the theoretical frameworks surrounding hysteria, necessitating a vigilant critique of these historical transformations (Illis, 2002).

Ultimately, the exploration of evolving theories and philosophies related to hysteria provides an encompassing understanding of its intricate essence. By untangling the historical complexities, valuable insights into the cultural, medical, and philosophical dimensions that have shaped the perception of hysteria across the ages can be gleaned (Bustos et al., 2014).

Influential Medical Figures in Hysteria's History

Throughout history, many medical figures have significantly impacted the understanding and treatment of hysteria. **Hippocrates**: Often called the 'Father of Medicine', he described 'hysteria' as stemming from the uterus movement within a woman's body (Micale, 1996). His theories laid the foundation for the concept of hysteria and shaped medical discourse for centuries. **Paracelsus**: In the Renaissance era, this Swiss physician challenged the traditional views by attributing hysteria to an imbalance of bodily fluids instead of solely linking it to the uterus, indicating an evolving understanding of the disorder (Carveth & Carveth, 2004).

Jean-Martin Charcot: A prominent neurologist in the 19th century, Charcot researched hysteria at the Salpêtrière Hospital in Paris. His clinical observations aimed to establish hysteria as a legitimate neurological condition, distinct from psychological issues (Cramer, 2018). **Sigmund Freud**: The father of psychoanalysis, Freud significantly influenced the discourse on hysteria. His study of psychosexual development, particularly through the case of Anna O., provided insights into the disorder's psychodynamic aspects (Paster, 2017). **Joseph Breuer**: Collaborating with Freud, Breuer's pioneering work solidified the foundations of psychoanalytic theory concerning hysteria (Cramer, 2018). These figures laid the groundwork for ongoing debates on the intersection of biology, psychology, and culture in medical perceptions. Their legacies continue to affect modern mental health approaches, fostering advancements in psychiatry and neurology (Cramer, 2018).

Cultural Interpretations and Misunderstandings

Cultural perceptions have historically shaped the understanding of hysteria (Showalter, 2018): **Societal Attitudes**: Cultural views often reflected societal attitudes toward women, influencing how hysteria was diagnosed and treated. In some cultures, hysteria was linked to supernatural forces or divine punishment, leading to stigmatization (Tasca et al., 2012). **Spiritual Perspectives**: Conversely, other cultures saw hysteria as spiritual enlightenment or a reaction to oppressive norms, highlighting a variety of interpretations (Layne, 2019). **Colonial Influences**: Colonial encounters and cultural exchanges added layers of misunderstanding, complicating the discourse on hysteria and contributing to disparities in diagnosis and care (Micale, 1996). **Media Representation**: Popular media and artistic representations often sensationalize hysteria, reinforcing stereotypes and hindering nuanced understanding (Bustos et al., 2014).

Examining these cultural implications is crucial for recognizing their impact on individuals with hysteria. By addressing these issues, we can promote empathy and accurate representation in mental health discussions, leading to culturally sensitive approaches to diagnosis and treatment (Cramer, 2018).

The Transition from Historical to Modern Viewpoints

The journey of hysteria reveals a critical transition from historical to modern perspectives, emphasizing scientific and empathetic understanding (Paster, 2017): **Reevaluation of Hysteria**: This shift reflects a growing recognition of mental health complexities and society's role in misinterpretations, moving away from stigmatizing views. **Advancements in Medical Practices**: As understanding of psychological conditions has evolved, emotional distress is no longer merely pathologized as 'hysterics'. This fosters compassionate treatment approaches (Cramer, 2018). **Cultural Renaissance**: The changing cultural landscape, influenced by literature, art, and media, has fostered positive shifts in attitudes towards hysteria, embracing nuanced depictions and destigmatizing experiences (Showalter, 2018).

As we navigate this transition, it's essential to confront residual historical prejudices. Acknowledging these challenges is vital for ensuring that outdated beliefs do not persist in modern ideologies. By doing so, we can create an environment characterized by compassion, understanding, and equitable healing opportunities for those affected by hysteria. In reflecting on this transition, we perpetuate advocacy for a future where stigma is eradicated, replaced by empathy and enlightened progression (Illis, 2002).

Impact on Society and Medical Practice

The impact of hysteria on both society and medical practice has been profound, shaping perceptions of mental health and influencing how professionals diagnose and treat related conditions (Tasca et al., 2012): **Societal Stigmatization**: Historically, hysteria was often used to dismiss women's legitimate emotional and physical distress, perpetuating stereotypes about female weakness. This led to societal expectations that undermined the seriousness of women's health issues (Paster, 2017). **Diagnostic Procedures and Treatment**: The mischaracterization of hysteria has resulted in overmedication, misdiagnosis, and underdiagnosis, particularly for mental health issues prevalent in women (Bustos et al., 2014). Outdated perceptions obstructed the development of effective treatments for these disorders. **Disparities in Care**: The gendered nature of hysteria has contributed to inequities in mental health care, with many women receiving inadequate treatment and support. This highlights the urgent need to reevaluate historical biases (Illis, 2002). **Call for Reevaluation**: Addressing these challenges calls for a comprehensive understanding of hysteria's historical implications. Medical professionals must improve the diagnosis and treatment of disorders previously linked to hysteria, avoiding stereotypes and fostering a balanced, empathetic approach (Micale, 1996). **Cultural Perspective**: Building a more inclusive understanding of mental health is critical for mitigating the stigma associated with hysteria and promoting an environment that supports effective treatment for all individuals (Cramer, 2018).

Reflection on Historical Missteps

Reflecting on historical missteps regarding hysteria reveals significant patterns that have shaped current understanding (Showalter, 2018): **Pathologization of Women's Experiences**: The association of hysteria with women led to biases in diagnosis and treatment, resulting in invasive procedures and a lack of respect for women's autonomy (Illis, 2002). **Misinterpretation of Symptoms**: Historical interpretations, such as the 'wandering womb' theory, exemplify a narrow perspective that disregards the biological, psychological, and social factors contributing to hysteria, hindering effective intervention development (Paster, 2017). **Influential Figures**: While influential, medical pioneers like Charcot and Freud propagated misconceptions that reinforced societal stigma. Critical analysis of their contributions highlights the need for scrutiny in medical history (Cramer, 2018). **Call to Action**: Reflecting on these missteps emphasizes the need for inclusive, evidence-based approaches that prioritize individual well-being and agency. This introspection is crucial for fostering empathy and effectiveness in addressing hysteria (Bustos et al., 2014).

In a Nutshell:

Introduction to Hysteria: Past and Present

Hysteria, a term derived from the Greek word "hystera" meaning uterus, has a long and complex history that intertwines with the evolution of medical science, psychology, and cultural perceptions of gender and mental health. The earliest references to hysteria can be traced back to ancient Egyptian medical papyri around 1900 B.C., where it was attributed to the movement of the uterus within the body, causing various physical and mental symptoms. This concept was further developed by Greek physicians such as Hippocrates and Galen, who linked the disorder to the female reproductive system and sexual deprivation.

During the Renaissance, hysteria was often interpreted as a sign of demonic possession, leading to treatments involving exorcism and even torture. The Enlightenment brought a shift towards more scientific explanations, with figures like Thomas Willis and Robert Whytt proposing neurological and physiological causes. The 19th century marked a significant period in the study of hysteria, with Jean-Martin Charcot and Sigmund Freud making substantial contributions. Charcot's work at the Salpêtrière Hospital in Paris and Freud's development of psychoanalysis were pivotal in shaping modern understandings of the disorder.

Despite these advancements, hysteria remained a controversial and often misunderstood condition. The 20th century saw a decline in the diagnosis of hysteria, partly due to changes in medical classifications and the rise of new psychological theories. The Diagnostic and Statistical Manual of Mental Disorders (DSM) eventually removed hysteria as a distinct diagnosis, reflecting a broader shift towards more specific and scientifically grounded categories of mental illness.

In contemporary times, the concept of hysteria has evolved, with some scholars arguing that modern conditions such as chronic fatigue syndrome, multiple personality disorder, and Gulf War syndrome represent new forms of hysteria influenced by cultural and societal factors. This ongoing evolution highlights the complex interplay between medical science, cultural narratives, and the human experience of mental health.

The study of hysteria offers valuable insights into the history of medicine, the development of psychological theories, and the cultural construction of gender and mental illness. As we continue to explore and understand this multifaceted disorder, it remains a testament to the enduring challenge of deciphering the intricate relationship between mind and body.

References For Further Reading

Bailey, P. (1966). Hysteria: The History of a Disease. Archives of General Psychiatry, 14, 332-333. https://doi.org/10.1001/ARCHPSYC.1966.01730090108024.

Bustos, E., Galli, S., Haffen, E., & Moulin, T. (2014). Clinical manifestations of hysteria: an epistemological perspective or how historical dynamics illuminate current practice.. Frontiers of neurology and neuroscience, 35, 28-43. https://doi.org/10.1159/000360436.

Carveth, D., & Carveth, J. (2004). Fugitives from Guilt: Postmodern De-Moralization and the New Hysterias. American Imago, 60, 445 - 479. https://doi.org/10.1353/AIM.2004.0002.

Cramer, P. (2018). What Has Happened to Hysteria? Journal of Nervous & Mental Disease. https://doi.org/10.1097/NMD.0000000000000850.

Illis, L. (2002). Hysteria. Spinal Cord, 40, 311-312. https://doi.org/10.1038/sj.sc.3101327.

Layne, M. (2019). A SHORT "HISTORY" OF HYSTERIA. Approaching Hysteria. https://doi.org/10.1515/9780690119 4486-004.

Lerner, P. (2010). Andrew Scull, Hysteria: the biography, Biographies of Disease Series, Oxford University Press, 2009.

Micale, M. (1989). Hysteria and its Historiography: A Review of Past and Present Writings (I). History of Science, 27, 223 - 261. https://doi.org/10.1177/007327538902700301.

Micale, M. (1996). Approaching Hysteria: Disease and Its Interpretations. https://doi.org/10.2307/2169471.

Paster, G. (2017). Hysteria: A very short introduction. Oxford University Press.

Showalter, E. (2018). The female malady: Women, madness, and English culture, 1830-1980. Virago Press.

Tasca, C., Rapetti, M., Carta, M., & Fadda, B. (2012). Women And Hysteria In The History Of Mental Health. Clinical Practice and Epidemiology in Mental Health: CP & EMH, 8, 110 - 119. https://doi.org/10.2174/1745017901208010110.

CHAPTER TWO

ANCIENT ORIGINS: THE WANDERING WOMB THEORY

Historical Context and Cultural Beliefs

Throughout antiquity, cultural beliefs significantly shaped the understanding of physical and mental health. In ancient societies, notions about anatomy, physiology, and psychosomatic disorders were deeply intertwined with religious, mythological, and philosophical influences. Early medical knowledge and healing practices were often rooted in a mythical and ritualistic context, where divine intervention was believed to both cause and cure afflictions. A pivotal aspect of early medical understanding was the concept of humoral theory, which posited that the human body's balance depended on the equilibrium of bodily fluids (Risse, 1988; Giancola & Garcia, 2022). This belief had profound implications for interpreting and treating various ailments, including those associated with what would later be recognized as symptoms of hysteria.

The exploration of societal views on gender roles and female physiology is essential for understanding historical health concepts. Ancient medical writings often reflected prevailing gender biases, shaping perceptions of women's health and afflictions (Cadden, 1993). To illuminate the foundational influences on the concept of the wandering womb, it is crucial to delve into the cultural underpinnings that informed early medical theory and practice. By examining this context, we gain insights into the complex landscape that has historically influenced interpretations of women's health and emotional well-being.

The Origins of the Wandering Womb Concept

The concept of the wandering womb, referred to as *hystera* in ancient Greek medicine, was a significant idea in the history of gynecology and women's health. It stemmed from the notion that the uterus was a mobile entity within a woman's body, leading to various physical and emotional disturbances. This concept can be traced back to ancient physicians and philosophers who sought to explain women's experiences from cultural and mythological perspectives (Dixon, 1994).

The wandering womb was intertwined with broader frameworks of early medical understanding, shaping perceptions of women's health for centuries. The idea underscored the belief that a woman's emotional and physical states could be influenced by the position of her reproductive organs, challenging and complicating how ailments specific to women were interpreted and treated (Hurst, 1983).

Mythological Underpinnings: Influence of Ancient Texts

In ancient cultures, the understanding of female reproductive health was deeply connected to mythological beliefs and narratives. The portrayal of women's bodies and their related ailments in ancient texts played a foundational role in shaping societal perceptions and medical ideologies. Myths frequently depicted women's health as linked to divine or supernatural forces, attributing conditions like the wandering womb to otherworldly causes (Dmytriw, 2014).

In various ancient civilizations—Greek, Roman, Egyptian, and Mesopotamian—narratives often referenced the restless or displaced uterus as a source of women's physical and mental distress. These mythological narratives not only influenced early medical thought but also perpetuated enduring misconceptions about women's health. The symbolic representations of the womb entrenched notions of female vulnerability and irrationality, contributing to the stigmatization and marginalization of women in both medical and societal domains (Preez, 2004).

By exploring these influential texts, we can gain insights into the origins of beliefs surrounding women's reproductive health and their impact on subsequent medical practices and societal attitudes. The interplay between mythology, culture, and medicine significantly influenced how female-specific ailments were perceived and treated in early medical literature and practice (Layne, 2019).

Philosophical Interpretations in Greek Medicine

The ancient Greeks made remarkable contributions to medicine, laying the groundwork for Western medical knowledge.

Philosophical interpretations shaped Greek medicine, reflecting the deep connection between philosophical and medical ideas (Dmytriw, 2014). Figures like Hippocrates and Galen introduced concepts that influenced medical practice for centuries.

Central to Greek medicine was the idea of balance—specifically, the equilibrium among various bodily humors. This concept derived from a broader philosophical notion of harmony and moderation, encapsulated in the famous aphorism "Παν μέτρον άριστον" (*Pan metron ariston*), meaning "Everything in moderation" (Geetha & Channabasavanna, 1981). These philosophical underpinnings guided the diagnostic and therapeutic approaches of ancient Greek physicians, emphasizing the restoration of humoral equilibrium as essential for health (Dmytriw, 2014).

Additionally, the philosophical school of naturalism, advocated by thinkers like Empedocles and later Hippocratic physicians, posited that the human body is composed of the four elements: earth, water, air, and fire. This elemental theory suggested a holistic integration of the individual with the natural world. Humoral imbalances were perceived as disruptions in cosmic harmony, aligning with philosophical views of the interconnectedness of all things (Hurst, 1983).

Greek philosophical thought also contributed to the ethical dimensions of medical practice. The Hippocratic Oath, embodying moral principles, reflected the commitment of physicians to confidentiality, moral integrity, and utilizing their skills for the benefit of humanity (Hurst, 1983). This ethical foundation resonates with the values espoused by Greek philosophers such as Socrates and Plato. Furthermore, philosophical schools like the Peripatetics and Stoics prompted discussions on the mind-body relationship. This holistic approach recognized that well-being encompassed not just physical health but also mental and emotional equilibrium, influencing medical treatments (Giancola & Garcia, 2022).

In summary, the philosophical interpretations in Greek medicine provided a comprehensive understanding of health and illness, with an enduring influence that resonates in contemporary medical ethics and holistic healthcare approaches. The pursuit of balance and harmony in human well-being remains a lasting legacy of ancient medical and philosophical thought.

Role of Egyptian and Mesopotamian Practices

Insights into Medical Beliefs
Ancient Egyptian and Mesopotamian medical practices significantly contributed to the historical foundations of medical beliefs and practices related to female health. In both civilizations, healthcare was deeply intertwined with religious and spiritual beliefs, leading to a holistic approach that considered the physical, spiritual, and supernatural aspects of well-being (Riddle, 1992). Women's health held a paramount place in these societies, as evidenced by various medical texts and artifacts that attest to the careful consideration given to gynecological issues and the understanding of female anatomy as distinct from male.

Medical Practices in Ancient Egypt

In Ancient Egypt, medical knowledge was largely fostered within the temples, where priests often acted as physicians. The Ebers Papyrus, dated to around 1550 BCE, is one of the oldest known medical texts and contains detailed descriptions of numerous diseases and their treatments, including those specific to women. Egyptians recognized the uterus's central role in women's health, aligning with later concepts, such as the Wandering Womb Theory, which suggested that the uterus could cause various ailments if it became displaced (Dmytriw, 2014).

Additionally, ancient Egyptians employed sophisticated methods for treating gynecological conditions, such as the use of pessaries and various herbal remedies (Geetha & Channabasavanna, 1981). Some references in medical texts indicate an advanced understanding of female anatomy and reproductive health, suggesting treatments that addressed conditions like infertility and menstrual irregularities with a degree of care that resonates even today.

Medical Practices in Mesopotamia

Similarly, in Mesopotamia, medical knowledge was deeply rooted in religious practices. The line between divine intervention and medical treatment often blurred, as numerous incantations and rituals were performed alongside physical remedies (Risse, 1988). The diagnostic techniques included careful bodily observation, divination, and empirical observations, indicating a complex understanding of the human body and health.

Mesopotamian texts also referenced obstetrical practices, focusing on conditions such as infertility, miscarriage, and menstrual disorders. These records show that Mesopotamia, like Egypt, placed significant emphasis on women's health, often addressing these concerns through a combination of ritualistic practices and empirical methods (Giancola & Garcia, 2022).

Holistic Approach to Healthcare

Both Egyptian and Mesopotamian medical practices were characterized by a deep reverence for the mysteries of the human body. They sought to address ailments through a balance of physical, spiritual, and supernatural means, recognizing that health was a multifaceted concept (Shetty et al., 2020). This holistic approach laid a foundational understanding that would influence subsequent cultures and the evolution of medical theories and practices.

The treatment methods employed by these ancient civilizations, which included herbal remedies, ritualistic healing, and spiritual interventions, continue to inform contemporary discussions

about women's health, particularly regarding conditions historically associated with hysteria. The significance of women's health
in these ancient frameworks established important cultural prece-
dents that echo through time.

Aristotle and Hippocrates: Foundational Theories

Aristotle's Contributions

In the tapestry of ancient medical history, the contributions of
Aristotle and Hippocrates stand as bedrocks for our understanding of health and illness (Shetty et al., 2020). Aristotle's work in
biology and human anatomy marked a pivotal shift in medical
knowledge. He proposed the concept of the four humors—blood,
phlegm, yellow bile, and black bile—which became foundational
in medical diagnosis and treatment practices for centuries.

Aristotle's emphasis on empirical observation and systematic
classification established a precursor to scientific inquiry in medicine. By advocating for observation over mythological explanations, Aristotle set the stage for a more methodical approach to
understanding health and disease (Dmytriw, 2014).

Hippocrates and Medical Ethics

Meanwhile, Hippocrates, often dubbed the "Father of Medicine,"
introduced fundamental ethical standards and rational methodologies for medical practice. His approach emphasized the interconnectedness of mind, body, and the environment, advocating
for individualized treatment and preventive care (Dixon, 1994).
The Hippocratic Oath, outlining ethical principles that prioritize
patient welfare, remains influential in modern medical ethics.

Hippocrates diverged from previous medical paradigms by rejecting supernatural explanations for disease. His endorsement of naturalistic explanations marked a significant shift towards what we now recognize as evidence-based medicine. His teachings stressed that illness was a result of natural factors rather than divine punishments (Hurst, 1983).

Enduring Legacy

The theories of Aristotle and Hippocrates permeated not only the field of medicine but also philosophical discourse, shaping societal perceptions of health and illness. Their commitment to empirical methods, ethical considerations, and holistic approaches laid the groundwork for medical education and practice that continues to resonate today.

Diagnosis and Treatment Methods in Antiquity

Intertwining of Diagnosis and Cultural Beliefs

In the ancient world, the diagnosis and treatment of ailments—particularly those linked to the Wandering Womb Theory—were deeply intertwined with the cultural and societal beliefs of the time. Medical practitioners utilized a combination of empirical observations, philosophical ideas, and mythological interpretations to address health concerns (Dmytriw, 2014). The understanding of the human body and its afflictions frequently incorporated spiritual or supernatural beliefs.

Diagnostic Methods in Antiquity

Primary diagnostic methods in antiquity included:

- **Observation of Symptoms**: Careful monitoring of physical signs and symptoms.

- **Palpation**: Physical examination of the body to identify abnormalities.

- **Patient Inquiry**: Gathering medical histories from patients to understand their ailments.

However, these diagnostic practices were often influenced by superstitions and limited scientific understanding, leading to varying interpretations of health conditions.

Treatment Approaches

Treatment methods for conditions related to the Wandering Womb Theory reflected the modalities of the era, which included:
- **Herbal Remedies**: Utilizing natural plants and herbs for healing properties.

- **Dietary Adjustments**: Modifying food intake to restore health.

- **Ritualistic Incantations**: Employing prayers, spells, and rituals to address spiritual aspects of health (Catonné et al., 1992).

In particular, treatments often included:
- **Physical Manipulation**: Certain practices involved repositioning the uterus, believed necessary to restore it to its rightful place.

- **Aromatic Therapies**: The use of scents and essential oils was thought to help in calming or redefining the uterus's position.

While primitive by today's standards, these treatment techniques represented the earnest efforts of ancient healers striving to address the perceived conditions affecting women. The cultural significance and symbolism of these practices provide valuable insights into the ancient mindset and their understanding of health and the human body.

Criticism and Acceptance through Ancient Societies

Spectrum of Perspectives on Hysteria

In exploring the historical context of hysteria, it is essential to examine the various degrees of criticism and acceptance across different ancient societies. The concept of hysteria, often associated with the wandering womb theory, evoked diverse responses from influential thinkers and communities in Greece, Rome, Egypt, and Mesopotamia (Dixon, 1994).

Greek Attitudes Towards Hysteria

Among the ancient Greeks, philosophers like Plato and Aristotle held differing views on hysteria's legitimacy. Plato linked hysteria to physical ailments involving the uterus, while Aristotle regarded it as originating from psychological disturbances (Geetha & Channabasavanna, 1981). These competing perspectives influenced medical practice, shaping how physicians diagnosed and treated individuals exhibiting hysterical symptoms.

Roman Contributions to Understanding Hysteria

In Roman society, physicians such as Galen further developed and critiqued existing theories of hysteria, merging practical observation with philosophical inquiry. While advances in medical knowledge continued, prevailing gender biases, rooted in patriarchal views, contributed to the reinforcement of the wandering womb theory, perpetuating societal attitudes about women's health (Risse, 1988).

Egyptian and Mesopotamian Pragmatism

In contrast, Egyptian and Mesopotamian cultures adopted a more pragmatic approach to hysteria. Their medical practitioners combined observation with ritualistic treatments to alleviate symptoms of hysteria. Although their methods were steeped in spirituality, these societies aimed to mitigate suffering while attempting to understand the complexities of women's health (Shetty et al., 2020).

Conclusion and Historical Reflection

The juxtaposition of these varying attitudes demonstrates a complex interplay of cultural, religious, and medical factors that shaped ancient societies' perceptions of hysteria. Some embraced divine explanations, while others sought rational, empirical approaches. Recognizing the diverse responses to hysteria enriches our understanding of its historical evolution and its impact on subsequent medical and societal developments. Understanding the criticism and acceptance within ancient civilizations lays the groundwork for contextualizing contemporary dialogues on women's health and the lingering consequences of historical perceptions.

Case Studies of Recorded Instances

Historical Perspectives on Hysteria

The exploration of historical case studies offers valuable insights into the perceptions and treatments of hysteria across ancient societies. Through the examination of medical history, we come across an array of narratives that illuminate the multifaceted nature of this enigmatic condition. These recorded instances from different civilizations provide a glimpse into the diverse manifestations of symptoms attributed to hysteria, as well as the societal responses to these symptoms. By meticulously evaluating these case studies, we can discern patterns, challenges, and prevailing attitudes surrounding hysteria.

Ancient Egyptian Accounts

In ancient Egypt, historical records, particularly those found in medical papyri, allude to individuals exhibiting symptoms aligning with what would today be interpreted as hysteria. The Ebers Papyrus, one of the most significant medical texts from this period, outlines a variety of physical and psychological symptoms in women, suggesting that physicians of the time recognized conditions that may now be categorized as hysterical (Riddle, 1992). One account describes a woman experiencing intense emotional distress, unexplained physical complaints, and episodes of fainting. Such symptoms may have been perceived as stemming from spiritual disturbances or imbalances in bodily humors. Treatments mentioned in the texts included herbal remedies, rituals for divine favor, and guidance from priest-physicians who played dual roles in medicine and religion, indicating a holistic approach to understanding and treating women's health issues.

Mesopotamian Records

Similarly, Mesopotamian records present instances where individuals exhibited perplexing symptoms that can be construed as hysterical. Tablets from this civilization often recount cases of women experiencing fits of crying, seizures, and cognitive disturbances, which could be linked to the societal stressors and expectations faced by women at that time. These symptoms were typically treated through a combination of herbal medicines and incantations intended to appease the gods or to cleanse the afflicted individual of evil spirits (Catonné et al., 1992).

The Diagnostic Handbook of the ancient Mesopotamians illustrates the intersection of medicine and magic, where physical ailments were addressed through a spiritual lens. One notable case involved a woman whose symptoms included erratic behavior and intense emotional fluctuations; the prescribed treatment combined practical remedies, such as dietary changes, with ritualistic practices aimed at restoring her mental and spiritual balance.

The Influence of Aristotle and Hippocrates

The writings of scholars such as Aristotle and Hippocrates also contribute significantly to the historical discourse on hysteria. They documented detailed observations of patients exhibiting symptoms now associated with hysteria, reflecting on the variability of these symptoms and the social context surrounding their care. Aristotle, for instance, theorized that women were more predisposed to certain emotional disturbances because of their unique physiological makeup, notably the influence of the uterus on their emotional well-being (Geetha & Channabasavanna, 1981). His observations contributed to the understanding of hysteria as a condition linked to both physical and psychological factors.

Hippocrates further advanced these ideas, rejecting supernatural explanations in favor of a more systematic and professional approach to medicine. He is often credited with providing the first clinical descriptions of what might be classified as hysterical symptoms, emphasizing the importance of clinical observation and the interplay between the body and emotions (Hurst, 1983).

Social and Cultural Implications

These recorded instances reveal a complex intersection of beliefs, perceptions, and medical interventions related to hysteria. The narratives illustrate how societal attitudes towards women's health—deeply influenced by cultural, religious, and philosophical beliefs—shaped the diagnostic and treatment strategies employed in ancient civilizations. The variability in symptoms and their interpretations underscores the evolving terminology and understanding of this complex phenomenon.

The legacy of these case studies enriches our comprehension of the historical complexities surrounding hysteria, which not only affected the lives of individuals but also had profound implications for the communities to which they belonged. As we examine the continuum of documented case studies, we uncover a compelling narrative that transcends time and geography, providing a panoramic view of the evolution of hysteria and its treatment across civilizations.

Legacy and Transition into Medieval Concepts

The Wandering Womb's Enduring Influence

The legacy of the Wandering Womb theory from ancient times significantly impacted the conceptualization of women's health as societies transitioned into the medieval period (Dmytriw, 2014). The early theories and practices of ancient civilizations laid a foundational understanding of gynecology, which continued to evolve as new religious and scholarly perspectives emerged.

Integration of Theology and Philosophy

During the medieval period, the integration of Christian theology with Greek philosophical ideals resulted in a complex amalgamation of beliefs regarding women's bodies and reproductive health. The concept of the wandering womb persisted, now enriched by theological doctrines and the teachings of prominent scholars like Galen and Avicenna. Medical treatises and manuscripts from this era reflected the enduring legacy of ancient gynecological theories, often merging traditional practices with evolving intellectual frameworks (Dmytriw, 2014).

Both Galen and Avicenna contributed significantly to medical knowledge, with Galen's works synthesizing previous understandings and Avicenna introducing new ideas about anatomy and the nature of diseases (Risse, 1988). Their writings perpetuated foundational concepts from antiquity while offering a new framework for understanding human health.

Medical Institutions and the Role of Healers

The transition to medieval concepts also saw the proliferation of medical institutions where physicians and healers sought to reconcile teachings from antiquity with emergent medieval understandings of anatomy and physiology. The institutionalization of medical knowledge allowed for the dissemination of both traditional and innovative theories regarding women's health.

Moreover, female healers and midwives emerged as crucial figures in administering care to women during this period. These practitioners operated at the intersection of empirical practices and inherited knowledge, reflecting a dualistic nature in medical practices. Their expertise in childbirth, reproductive health, and herbal remedies is a testament to the ongoing relevance of ancient practices while adapting to changing cultural landscapes (Shetty et al., 2020).

Scholastic Culture and Women's Health Debates

Additionally, the burgeoning scholastic culture of medieval Europe fostered rich debates and commentaries on women's bodies, fertility, and the implications of the wandering womb theory. Notable figures such as Hildegard of Bingen and Trotula de Ruggiero engaged in discussions that addressed the physiological and metaphysical aspects of women's health (Layne, 2019). Hildegard's writings, which explored the intertwining of spirituality and health, highlighted the connection between emotional states and physical well-being. Trotula's medical texts specifically catered to women's health, offering insights into gynecological issues and reflecting a growing acknowledgment of the unique health needs of women.

Conclusion: Historical Continuity and Evolving Paradigms

Ultimately, the legacy of the wandering womb theory and its evolution during the medieval period underscores the intricate interplay between historical continuity and changing paradigms of women's health. The persistence and adaptation of ancient gynecological beliefs within medieval frameworks laid the foundation for future developments in understanding and treating female-specific ailments.

This historical trajectory highlights how entrenched beliefs can evolve, influencing subsequent generations of medical practice. Through the exploration of these ideas and practices, we trace the roots of contemporary gynecological discourse and reflect on how historical attitudes toward women's health continue to shape modern understandings. This journey through time reveals the profound impact of hysteria as a medical and cultural concept, illustrating its legacy in the ongoing study of health and disease.

In a Nutshell:

Ancient Origins of Hysteria: The Wandering Womb Theory

The concept of hysteria, particularly the "wandering womb" theory, has its roots in ancient medical traditions. This theory posited that a woman's uterus could move freely within her body, causing various physical and psychological symptoms. This idea has evolved significantly over time, influenced by cultural, medical, and social changes.

Key Insights from Research Papers

- **Origins and Early Descriptions**:
  - The wandering womb theory originated in ancient Egypt and was later adopted by Greek physi-

cians in the fourth century B.C. They described various symptoms believed to be caused by a restless uterus.

○ The term "hysteria" is derived from the Greek word "hystera," meaning womb. Plato and other ancient Greek thinkers expanded on this idea, suggesting that an under-stimulated uterus could cause a range of diseases by wandering through the body.

- **Symptoms and Treatments**:

  ○ Ancient descriptions of hysteria included a wide range of symptoms such as anxiety, faintness, and muscle spasms. Treatments often involved methods to lure the uterus back to its proper place, including pelvic massage, sneezing, and vigorous physical activities.

  ○ The Greeks believed that prolonged sexual continence could lead to hysteria, a view that influenced medical thought for centuries.

- **Evolution of the Concept**:

  ○ Over time, the understanding of hysteria evolved. By the 19th century, it was seen as a condition with no anatomical basis, often described as a simulacrum of symptoms without a clear bodily referent.

  ○ The concept of hysteria has been redefined multiple times, from a wandering womb to demonic possession, and later to neurological and psychological disorders. Today, it is recognized under terms like functional neurological disorders and somatization disorders.

- **Cultural and Social Influences**:

  - Cultural and social contexts have heavily influenced the perception and treatment of hysteria. For instance, in the 18th and 19th centuries, hysteria was often linked to sexual dissatisfaction and treated with methods aimed at addressing this perceived cause.

  - The medicalization of female sexuality and the pathologization of normal female behaviors were significant aspects of the historical treatment of hysteria.

Conclusion

The wandering womb theory of hysteria has a long and complex history, originating in ancient Egypt and evolving through Greek, medieval, and modern medical thought. Initially attributed to a physically wandering uterus, the concept of hysteria has been reinterpreted over the centuries to reflect changing medical, cultural, and social understandings. Today, while the term "hysteria" is no longer used in modern medical classifications, its historical journey highlights the interplay between medical theories and societal attitudes towards women's health.

References

Cadden, J. (1993). Meanings of sex: The culture of the uterus and the history of female disease in early modern England. Routledge.

Catonné Jp et al. (1992). Hippocratic concept of hysteria. Annales médico-psychologiques, 150, 705-719.

Dixon, L. (1994). Beware the wandering womb–painterly reflections of early gynecological theory. Cancer Investigation, 12 1, 66–73.

Dmytriw, A. (2014). Gender and Sex Manifestations in Hysteria Across Medicine and the Arts. European Neurology, 73, 44 - 50. https://doi.org/10.1159/000367891.

Geetha, P., & Channabasavanna, S. (1981). A Study of Personality in Hysteria. Indian Journal of Psychological Medicine, 4, 65 - 69. https://doi.org/10.1177/0975156419810112.

Giancola, A., & Garcia, C. (2022). Hysteria: history of a conceptual and clinical pathomorphosis. European Psychiatry, 65, S545 - S546. https://doi.org/10.1192/j.eurpsy.2022.1397.

Hurst, L. (1983). Freud and the Great Neurosis: Discussion Paper. Journal of the Royal Society of Medicine, 76, 57 - 61. https://doi.org/10.1177/014107688307600113.

Layne, M. (2019). A SHORT "HISTORY" OF HYSTERIA. Approaching Hysteria. https://doi.org/10.1515/9780691194486-004.

Preez, A. (2004). Putting on appearances: Mimetic representations of hysteria. de arte, 39, 47 - 61. https://doi.org/10.1080/00043389.2004.11877020.

Riddle, J. M. (1992). Contraception and abortion from the ancient world to the Renaissance. Harvard University Press.

Risse, G. (1988). Hysteria at the Edinburgh Infirmary: the construction and treatment of a disease, 1770-1800.. Medical History, 32, 1 - 22. https://doi.org/10.1017/S0025727300047578.

Shetty, S., Chandini, S., Fernandes, S., & Safeekh, A. (2020). Hysteria: A historical perspective. Archives of Medicine and Health Sciences, 8, 312 - 315. https://doi.org/10.4103/amhs.amhs_220_20.

CHAPTER THREE

MEDIEVAL AND RENAISSANCE PERSPECTIVES ON HYSTERIA

The Cultural Context of Hysteria in the Middle Ages

To grasp the intricate perspective on hysteria during the Middle Ages, it is imperative to plunge into the multifaceted cultural milieu that defined this historical epoch. Medieval society was deeply permeated by its normative values and hierarchical constructs, with its social fabric intricately woven around the Church, aristocratic lineages, and the agrarian populace. These societal paradigms were instrumental in sculpting perceptions of health, illness, and notably, mental afflictions such as hysteria. Religious ideologies and dogmas significantly influence medical paradigms, often intermingling spiritual and corporeal rationalizations for maladies. The dominant belief that illness could be a manifestation of divine retribution or diabolical possession shaped the understanding of conditions like hysteria (Gurevich, 1994). Within this context, women were particularly susceptible to being deemed hysterical, a phenomenon exacerbated by the entrenched belief in their inherent moral frailty, which was codified through the biblical narrative of Eve's transgression (Tasca et al., 2012). Thus, the prevailing societal norms and ecclesiastical dogmas of the Middle Ages profoundly shaped the perception and management of individuals exhibiting symptoms reminiscent of hysteria. A meticulous inquiry into these historical influences allows for a clearer elucidation of the evolution of attitudes toward hysteria within the medieval framework.

The Interplay of Religious Beliefs and Medical Thought

The Middle Ages are characterized by the omnipresent influence of religious beliefs across all dimensions of life, including the realm of medical thought. Dominated by the doctrines of the Catholic Church, the prevailing worldview significantly shaped interpretations of health and ailment. Religious tenets framed perceptions of the corporeal form and its afflictions, attributing both somatic and psychological disorders to spiritual origins (Kroll, Bachrach, & Carey, 2002). The intertwining concepts of sin and divine chastisement permeated medical discourse, engendering the belief that illnesses, hysteria included, were frequently reflections of moral transgressions or manifestations of wicked spiritual entities. Consequently, the methodologies employed in treating hysteria became intricately enmeshed with religious practices and rituals. Religious figures played a pivotal role in the care of the afflicted, further blurring the distinctions between spiritual and physical remediation (Hłodzik et al., 2016). This convergence fostered the development of diverse therapeutic techniques, many of which incorporated prayers, exorcisms, and pilgrimages to sanctified sites. The reliance on religious interventions not only dictated the treatment of these individuals but also perpetuated societal stigma surrounding hysterical manifestations. Those displaying signs of hysteria often faced ostracism and condemnation as morally deficient, thereby exacerbating their distress and isolation (Ortega, 2012). Moreover, the profound association between religious convictions and medical thought impeded the emergence of more empirical methodologies to comprehend and address psychological and emotional turmoil. The amalgamation of religious doctrines with medical practices in the Middle Ages established a complex, often contentious legacy that continues to reverberate through contemporary perceptions and responses to psychological conditions.

Hysteria in Medieval Medical Canon

Throughout the medieval period, medical manuscripts emerged as pivotal repositories of knowledge, elucidating various ailments, including hysteria (Micale, 1989). Physicians and scholars from this era frequently referenced the venerable texts of ancient Greece and Rome, particularly those authored by Galen and Hippocrates, forming the foundation of their understanding of human ailments. However, it is essential to acknowledge that the prevailing notions of hysteria during this period were heavily modulated by contemporary cultural and religious ideologies. Many medieval medical treatises predominantly associated hysteria with women, often framing it through the lens of the 'wandering womb'—a belief with its origins rooted in ancient Greek thought (Layne, 2019). This 'wandering womb' theory posited that the uterus could migrate within a woman's anatomy, precipitating both physical and psychological disturbances. This belief endured throughout the medieval period and significantly influenced the narrative surrounding hysteria in medical literature. Medieval texts often depicted hysteria as a condition arising from instability or imbalance within the female reproductive system, leading to a tapestry of symptoms, including emotional turbulence, anxiety, and inexplicable somatic complaints (Gomes & Engelhardt, 2014). These manuscripts frequently portrayed the female body as intrinsically susceptible to such maladies due to its reproductive physiology. Furthermore, the confluence of religious ideologies with medical thought during this period was profound. The intersection of medical and spiritual discourses meant that the symptoms of hysteria were frequently interpreted through a moral and spiritual lens, with practitioners often viewing them as indicators of demonic possession or ethical failings (Zilboorg, 1935). As a result, the depiction of hysteria in medieval medical texts illustrates the intersection of ancient medical theories, gendered perceptions, and religious influences, all of which coalesced to shape societal interpretations of this intricate malady. While these representations might appear archaic by modern standards, they furnish essential insights into the historical construction of hysteria and its repercussions on individuals within medieval society.

Renaissance Transformations: From Humoral Theory to Empirical Observation

The Renaissance heralded substantial transformations in conceptualizing hysteria and other medical afflictions. This epoch signified a departure from the entrenched humoral theory, which attributed maladies to imbalances of bodily fluids, transitioning instead toward a more empirical approach grounded in observation and inquiry (Micale, 1996). Scholars and physicians began to scrutinize the long-cherished doctrines of ancient authorities, redirecting their focus to the meticulous examination and analysis of patients. This paradigm shift paved the way for significant advancements in the understanding and treatment modalities pertaining to hysteria. A salient advancement during this period was the heightened emphasis on clinical observation. Pioneering physicians such as Paracelsus and Vesalius eschewed the speculative aspects of traditional medical theories, opting instead for rigorous observation of symptoms and the human anatomical structure (Kroll et al., 2002). Their groundbreaking contributions laid the foundations for contemporary medical practices, greatly enhancing the development of a more evidence-based comprehension of hysteria. Additionally, the burgeoning field of anatomical studies, accompanied by dissection, offered unparalleled insights into the mechanics of the human body, thereby equipping physicians to transcend abstract theorization and engage with the tangible manifestations of hysteria. Esteemed anatomists like Andreas Vesalius challenged preexisting misconceptions regarding the female reproductive system, providing a more precise understanding of female anatomy that fundamentally altered attitudes toward hysteria (Hłodzik et al., 2016). Moreover, the Renaissance was marked by the ascent of individual scholars who played crucial roles in the discourse surrounding hysteria. Noteworthy figures such as Ambroise Paré and Girolamo Mercuriale enriched the field with fresh perspectives, blending empirical observations with their medical practices. Their meticulous documentation of case studies and patient experiences in the treatment of hysteria expanded the collective knowledge base and facilitated a more nuanced understanding of the condition (Gurevich, 1994). The efforts of these scholars paved the way for the development of therapeutic interventions that prioritized the individual's welfare and emphasized personalized care. In summation, the Renaissance era is a pivotal juncture in the historical narrative of hysteria, signaling a significant shift from age-old doctrines toward a milieu of empirical observation and scientific exploration. The invaluable contributions of preeminent figures, coupled with the rising focus on clinical scrutiny and anatomical investigation, established the groundwork for a more comprehensive understanding of hysteria and set the stage for subsequent advancements in the field of medicine.

Key Figures and Their Contributions to Hysteria

Many pivotal figures significantly advanced the understanding and treatment of hysteria during the Medieval and Renaissance epochs. Among these luminaries was Paracelsus, a Swiss physician who notably repudiated the dominant humoral theory in favor of chemical remedies, marking a paradigm shift in medical practices (Tasca et al., 2012). Paracelsus championed a holistic approach toward medicine, which facilitated a more progressive understanding of mental disorders, including hysteria, and laid the foundation for future innovations in psychiatric care. Another important figure was Trotula of Salerno, a pioneering female physician whose writings on gynecology and obstetrics critically challenged the prevailing attitudes toward women's health (Kroll et al., 2002). Her comprehensive texts provided invaluable insights into the manifestations and treatment of hysteria among women, directly contesting the entrenched patriarchal perspectives of her time. Additionally, Andreas Vesalius revolutionized anatomical studies, fundamentally altering the comprehension of the human body and thus enhancing the empirical approach to diagnosing and treating hysteria (Micale, 1996). His meticulous dissections and observations dismantled many ancient misconceptions, paving the way for more accurate medical interpretations. Moreover, the eminent philosopher and physician Marsilio Ficino played an instrumental role in advocating for a holistic perspective on mental health, underscoring the interconnection of mind, body, and spirit in treating hysteria (Micale, 1989). His work contributed to a broader philosophical framework harmonizing physical well-being with psychological health. Lastly, Johann Weyer, a Dutch physician and demonologist, deviated from the mainstream conviction that attributed hysteria to witchcraft. He fervently advocated for a more humane and rational understanding of mental disorders, emphasizing compassion over condemnation (Gomes

& Engelhardt, 2014). This critical stance helped shift the mental health dialogue, promoting ideas about care and understanding rather than alienation. Together, these key figures exemplify the evolution of thought regarding hysteria during the Medieval and Renaissance periods, encapsulating shifts in medical, philosophical, and societal attitudes instrumental in shaping modern understandings of mental health.

Gender, Witchcraft, and Hysteria

The connections between gender, witchcraft, and hysteria significantly influenced societal attitudes toward women's mental and physical health during the Medieval and Renaissance eras. The pervasive belief in women's inherent vulnerability and inferiority engendered the pathologization of behavior deemed deviant or nonconforming, which often included manifestations of hysteria as well as actions linked to alleged witchcraft (Tasca et al., 2012). The conflation of hysteria with witchcraft not only exacerbated the persecution of women but also framed their suffering as symptomatic of demonic possession or malevolent enchantment. This intersection of cultural, religious, and medical norms perpetuated the marginalization of women, reinforcing the notion of female hysteria as an expression of moral and spiritual decay (Layne, 2019). Furthermore, the widespread witch trials and accusations functioned as mechanisms of societal repression, effectively silencing women and entrenching gender-based power differentials (Ortega, 2012). The historical coupling of hysteria with witchcraft starkly illustrates how deeply embedded prejudices and fears shaped public perception, fostering environments ripe for the oppression of women throughout the Middle Ages and Renaissance. Critically examining this intersectionality is essential to understanding the lasting impact on mental health narratives and the ongoing struggle for gender equity and social justice. By acknowledging the historical roots of such damaging stereotypes and injustices, the contemporary discourse surrounding women's health can be reshaped to advocate for inclusive and empathetic approaches that address mental distress and its gendered implications.

Case Studies from the Medieval and Renaissance Era

Exploring the captivating history of hysteria during the Medieval and Renaissance periods necessitates examining specific case studies that illuminate prevailing perceptions and treatments of this enigmatic condition. One prominent figure is Margery Kempe, a medieval English mystic whose intense emotional and physical manifestations led to her labeling as "hysterical" by her contemporaries (Hłodzik et al., 2016). Kempe's experiences provide critical insight into the intersections of religious fervor, gender roles, and mental health during the medieval era. Another compelling case involves Hieronymus Bosch, the celebrated Dutch painter whose surreal and nightmarish artworks often reflected the societal prevalence of hysteria and other mental disturbances (Micale, 1996). Scholars hypothesize that Bosch's striking visual representations offer a unique lens through which the perception and interpretation of hysteria during the Renaissance can be analyzed, shaping societal attitudes toward mental distress. Additionally, the case of Isabella de Carazzi, a 16th-century Italian nun, illustrates the intricate overlap between spirituality and hysteria. Her recorded episodes of ecstatic visions and unexplainable bodily convulsions reveal the complexities in distinguishing divine experiences from psychological disorders, highlighting the delicate relationship between faith and mental well-being. Equally arresting is the narrative of King Charles VI of France, known as "Charles the Mad." His erratic behavior and profound melancholia have been scrutinized in light of modern psychological frameworks, providing fertile ground for debates among historians regarding the potential presence of underlying psychiatric conditions such as hysteria (Zilboorg, 1935). Analyzing King Charles's case enables a deeper understanding of how hysteria was perceived within royal circles and its broader implications for governance during that era. These varied case studies provide insight into the multifaceted nature of hysteria within the Medieval and Renaissance periods, revealing the intricate social, cultural, and medical dimensions of this complex affliction. By dissecting the narratives of individuals grappling with symptoms now associated with hysteria, we can enhance our comprehension of the historical intricacies that molded perceptions of mental health and illness.

Philosophical Interpretations of Mental Distress

Throughout the Medieval and Renaissance epochs, the concept of mental distress was profoundly intertwined with philosophical interpretations of the human condition. Scholars and philosophers grappled with mental anguish, frequently ascribing it to spiritual or moral deficiencies. The rigid hierarchical structure of society dictated a perspective wherein mental distress was construed as indicative of moral failings or divine punishment, deeply rooted in the era's religious convictions that prioritized spiritual and moral concerns (Kroll et al., 2002). A salient philosophical interpretation during this time emerged from the scholastic tradition, which sought to reconcile Christian theology with classical philosophy. Thinkers such as Thomas Aquinas and Augustine of Hippo profoundly influenced the development of a moral framework for understanding human emotions and behaviors (Micale, 1989). They posited that mental distress could be conceptualized through the prisms of sin and virtue, with diseases often interpreted as manifestations of spiritual deficiencies. Moreover, the

burgeoning interest in humanism during the Renaissance heralded a shift toward exploring individual experiences and emotions.
Philosophers like Michel de Montaigne and Erasmus of Rotter-
dam probed the complexities of human nature, emphasizing the
importance of introspection and self-awareness (Gurevich, 1994).
While these humanist thinkers did not specifically conceptualize
mental distress as a clinical issue, their works laid the groundwork for a nuanced exploration of emotional and psychological
experiences. The philosophical undercurrents regarding mental
distress also intersected with attitudes toward women during this
period. The concept of female hysteria, attributed to wandering
wombs and other perceived physiological instabilities, was shaped
by the philosophical view of women as inherently unstable and
emotionally volatile (Tasca et al., 2012). This prevailing perspective had significant ramifications for both medical treatment and
societal attitudes toward women exhibiting symptoms of mental
distress. Furthermore, the linkage between moral character and
mental well-being fostered the stigmatization and ostracization
of individuals experiencing psychological distress. The dominant
belief that mental suffering stemmed from personal failures often
led to severe judgment and social exclusion (Micale, 1996). The intertwining of philosophical interpretations with societal views on
mental distress had lasting impacts, shaping discourse surrounding
mental health for centuries to come.

Societal Impacts of Hysterical Diagnoses

The diagnosis of hysteria has historically been inextricably linked
with societal perceptions and attitudes toward women's mental
health (Layne, 2019). Throughout the medieval and Renaissance
periods, the implications of labeling women as hysterical extended
far beyond the confines of medical diagnoses, resonating throughout various societal structures. Such hysterical diagnoses reflect-

ed and reinforced prevailing cultural beliefs and norms, thereby entrenching gender inequalities. During these epochs, women deemed hysterical were often marginalized, their identities reduced to caricatures of emotional volatility (Tasca et al., 2012). This marginalization curtailed female agency and perpetuated stereotypes that depicted women as inherently weak and unstable. The notion that women were particularly susceptible to hysteria further entrenched their subjugation, casting their expressions of distress not as legitimate grievances but as manifestations of an intrinsically flawed disposition. Consequently, the societal dismissal of women's concerns hindered access to appropriate care and perpetuated broad patterns of stigmatization and discrimination. Moreover, the characterization of hysteria as predominantly a female ailment carried significant implications for social dynamics. It fostered an environment where women's valid concerns were trivialized, often dismissed as mere overreactions rather than thoughtful reactions to societal pressures and systemic inequities (Gurevich, 1994). This pervasive attitude thus not only stifled women's voices but also contributed to a culture that vilified and marginalized them. The socio-cultural ramifications of these diagnoses were further compounded by their connections to witchcraft and moral judgment. In an era steeped in superstition and religious doctrine, hysteria was often conflated with accusations of witchcraft (Kroll et al., 2002). This convergence of medical and moral discourse served to perpetuate stigma and justified severe repercussions for women labeled as hysterical. The historical interplay between female hysteria and witchcraft underscores a treacherous intersection of societal perception, medical diagnosis, and moral condemnation, often leading to persecution and ostracization. Additionally, the framing of hysteria within the context of moral judgment functioned as a mechanism for social control, effectively reinforcing existing power structures. By pathologizing women's emotional experiences, the diagnosis of hysteria acted as a tool for regulating female behavior and preserving patriarchal dominance

(Hłodzik et al., 2016). Women who diverged from established societal roles faced the risk of being labeled hysterical, which silenced
dissent and further entrenched conventional gender roles. In summary, the societal impacts of hysterical diagnoses during the medieval and Renaissance periods were multifaceted and profound,
permeating various aspects of social life. These impacts not only
shaped the experiences of individual patients but also influenced
broader societal attitudes toward women's mental health, perpetuating systemic inequalities and reinforcing normative standards
of femininity.

Transition to Enlightenment Thinking

The transition from the medieval and Renaissance periods to the
Age of Enlightenment marked a significant paradigm shift in societal perspectives and scientific methodologies. Characterized by
a move away from traditional and superstitious beliefs, the Enlightenment era emphasized rationalism, empiricism, and scientific inquiry (Micale, 1996). This intellectual awakening brought
notable changes to the understanding and treatment of mental
illnesses, including hysteria. In this context, Enlightenment thinking signified a departure from attributing women's mental distress solely to supernatural or religious phenomena. There was
a burgeoning emphasis on comprehending human behavior and
mental health through the lens of reason and natural laws. Influential philosophers such as René Descartes and John Locke laid
the groundwork for a new understanding of the mind and its disorders, positing that mental illnesses, including hysteria, could be
better understood as products of the human psyche rather than as
divine punishments or demonic possessions (Rushton, 2000). Enlightenment thinkers prioritized empirical observation and critical
analysis in the study of mental health. This intellectual climate
enabled the early emergence of psychiatry, fostering a gradual move

toward more humane treatment of individuals grappling with mental health issues characterized by symptoms that may have previously been labeled as hysteria. A pivotal development during this era was the establishment of the first psychiatric hospitals dedicated to the care and treatment of those experiencing mental illnesses (Ortega, 2012). The concept of moral treatment gained traction during the Enlightenment, emphasizing compassion, dignity, and individualized care for individuals with mental disorders (Hłodzik et al., 2016). This approach starkly contrasted with the harsh and stigmatizing practices that characterized earlier periods. Enlightenment philosophy encouraged a more kindhearted approach, recognizing the humanity of those afflicted by mental distress. Moreover, this era ushered in a broader exploration of alternative explanations for hysteria. Scholars began to redirect their focus from a narrow understanding rooted in female physiology and reproductive issues to considerations of environmental factors, societal conditions, and psychological stressors that could contribute to the manifestation of hysterical symptoms (Micale, 1996). This shift represented a critical advancement in the understanding of mental health, emphasizing the complex interplay of various influences. In conclusion, the transition to Enlightenment thinking signified a transformative moment in the conceptualization and treatment of hysteria. It advocated for greater compassion, scientific inquiry, and a holistic analysis of the societal variables influencing mental health. This period laid the groundwork for contemporary understandings of psychology, propelling society toward a more nuanced and informed discourse on mental well-being.

In a Nutshell:

Medieval and Renaissance Perspectives on Hysteria

The concept of hysteria has evolved significantly from ancient times through the medieval and Renaissance periods, reflecting broader cultural, medical, and social changes.

Medieval Mysticism and Hysteria

Modern psychiatrists and historians often linked medieval mysticism and asceticism to hysteria. These mystical states were sometimes dismissed as neurotic behaviors. However, it is crucial to understand these behaviors within their historical and cultural context rather than through the lens of modern Western standards. The association between mysticism and hysteria highlights the need to avoid value-laden diagnostic formulations when assessing historical personalities and behaviors.

Historical Evolution of Hysteria

Hysteria is one of the oldest diagnostic terms in medicine, with its origins tracing back to ancient Egypt and Greece. The term itself is derived from the Greek word "hystera," meaning womb, reflecting the early belief that the condition was related to the uterus. Over centuries, the understanding and treatment of hysteria evolved, with significant contributions from figures like Plato, Galen, and, later, Freud. During the medieval and Renaissance periods, hysteria was often linked to sexual deprivation and was treated with various methods, including pelvic massage and intercourse.

Witchcraft and Hysteria

The Renaissance period saw a significant overlap between the concepts of hysteria and witchcraft. Witchcraft persecutions were often manifestations of hysteria within European populations. Even after the peak of witchcraft fanaticism, sporadic outbursts of hysteria continued to occur, indicating the persistent nature of this condition in the cultural psyche of the time.

Psychogenic Disorders in the Middle Ages

In the Middle Ages, hysteria and related psychogenic disorders were sometimes seen as pathways to achieving ecstatic religious experiences. These conditions were not merely pathological but were also culturally significant, reflecting the enormous tension and repression of the time. The hysteria of this period was different from modern hysteria, affecting personalities who might not exhibit such tendencies today.

Women and Hysteria

Hysteria has historically been considered a female disorder, with its roots in both scientific and demonological perspectives. Over the centuries, it was treated with various methods, from herbal remedies to sexual therapies. The association of hysteria with sorcery led to severe punishments, including purification by fire. The understanding of hysteria continued to evolve, with significant changes occurring in the 20th century, leading to the decline of the diagnosis in Western medicine.

Cultural Interpretations of Hysteria

The interpretation of hysteria has varied widely across different historical periods and cultural contexts. From the wandering womb of ancient Greek medicine to the demonically possessed witches of the Renaissance, hysteria has been a powerful descriptive trope in various domains, including literature, art, and social thought. These cultural interpretations provide valuable insights into the broader cultural meanings of hysteria and its impact on society.

In summary, the perspectives on hysteria during the medieval and Renaissance periods were deeply intertwined with the cultural, religious, and medical beliefs of the time. Understanding these perspectives requires a nuanced approach that considers the historical context and avoids imposing modern diagnostic criteria on past behaviors and conditions.

References

Gallinek, A. (1942). PSYCHOGENIC DISORDERS AND THE CIVILIZATION OF THE MIDDLE AGES. American Journal of Psychiatry, 99, 42-54. https://doi.org/10.1176/AJP .99.1.42.

Gomes, M. M. M., & Engelhardt, E. (2014). A neurological bias in the history of hysteria: from the womb to the nervous system and Charcot. Arquivos de Neuro-Psiquiatria, 72 12, 972–975.

Gurevich, A. (1994). Medieval popular culture: Problems of belief and perception. Cambridge University Press.

Hłodzik, K., Dziwota, E., Karakuła-Juchnowicz, H., & Ola-jossy, M. (2016). The history of hysteria and what's next.... Current Problems of Psychiatry, 17, 31 - 37. https://doi.org/1 0.1515/cpp-2016-0005.

Kroll, J., Bachrach, B., & Carey, K. (2002). A reappraisal of medieval mysticism & hysteria. Mental Health, Religion & Culture, 5, 83 - 98. https://doi.org/10.1080/13674670110112749.

Layne, M. (2019). A SHORT "HISTORY" OF HYSTERIA. Approaching Hysteria. https://doi.org/10.1515/9780691194 486-004.

Micale, M. (1989). Hysteria and its Historiography: A Review of Past and Present Writings (I). History of Science, 27, 223 - 261. https://doi.org/10.1177/007327538902700301.

Micale, M. (1996). Approaching Hysteria: Disease and Its Interpretations. https://doi.org/10.2307/2169471.

Ortega, L. (2012). [New Forms of Hysteria: Globalization, Market and the Comeback of Hysteria]. Revista colombiana de psiquiatria, 41 3, 521-35. https://doi.org/10.1016/S0034-745 0(14)60026-3

Rushton, M. (2000). Symbolic blueprints: Women, medicine, and disease in medieval Europe. University of Exeter Press.

Tasca, C., Rapetti, M., Carta, M., & Fadda, B. (2012). Women And Hysteria In The History Of Mental Health. Clinical Practice and Epidemiology in Mental Health : CP & EMH, 8, 110 - 119. https://doi.org/10.2174/1745017901208010110.

Zilboorg, G. (1935). The Medical Man and the Witch during the Renaissance. Annals of Medical History, 7, 499 - 500. https://doi.org/10.2307/1415927.

CHAPTER FOUR

THE 19TH CENTURY BREAKTHROUGHS: CHARCOT AND FREUD

Historical Context: The Interplay of Medicine and Psychology in the 19th Century

The 19th century heralded a pivotal transformation in the comprehension of psychological disorders as the disciplines of medicine and psychology began to entwine in novel and substantive manners. This epoch bore witness to the emergence of avant-garde thinkers who established the foundational principles for contemporary neurology and psychology. As empirical knowledge burgeoned, the intricate nexus linking the brain, behavior, and mental well-being garnered unprecedented recognition (Micale, 1995). The intellectual milieu of this period was profoundly shaped by philosophical, cultural, and scientific currents, notably the Enlightenment, Romanticism, and the Industrial Revolution. At the confluence of these dynamic forces, both medical practitioners and scholars endeavored to delve into the complexities inherent to the human psyche.

The century also marked an evolution in the conceptualization of mental illness, transitioning from supernatural or religious interpretations to more systematic and empirical methodologies (Bogousslavsky, 2020). This paradigm shift catalyzed the nascent field of psychiatry, instigating a fundamental change in both the treatment and societal perception of psychological ailments. Concurrently, public attitudes towards mental health began to evolve, emphasizing compassion and scientific inquiry over stigmatization and dogma. The cross-disciplinary integration between neurology, psychiatry, and psychology facilitated a multifaceted investigation into mental disorders, paving the path for groundbreaking discoveries and theoretical advancements that resonate within modern practices today. The 19th century emerged as an undeniably transformative epoch where the convergence of medical and psychological insights paved the way for a profound understanding of the human mind's nuances.

Jean-Martin Charcot: A Luminary in Neurology

Jean-Martin Charcot emerges as a central figure in the annals of neurology, making consequential contributions to the elucidation of neurological disorders and the study of hysteria. Born in 1825, Charcot's foundational education and subsequent foray into medicine heralded the inception of a distinguished career that would ultimately mold the landscape of medical science (Oliveira et al., 2018). His unwavering commitment to rigorous research and clinical excellence positioned him as a preeminent authority in the domain of neuroscience during the 19th century. Charcot's transformative endeavors at the renowned Salpêtrière Hospital in Paris cemented his legacy as a pioneer in neurology. Through meticulous documentation and categorization of diverse neurological ailments, including multiple sclerosis and amyotrophic lateral sclerosis (ALS), he laid the groundwork for the systematic classification of these disorders.

Moreover, his inventive pedagogical methods and compassionate patient care solidified Salpêtrière as a bastion of medical innovation and scientific inquiry. One of his most enduring contributions lies in his pioneering investigations regarding hysterical phenomena. Charcot's scrupulous clinical observations sought to demystify the enigmatic symptoms and manifestations of hysteria, directly challenging the prevailing misconceptions and superstitions that clouded understanding of this disorder (Smith-Rosenberg, 2016). His rigorous approach to empirical evidence recast hysteria as a legitimate subject of scientific inquiry, ultimately paving the way for future advancements in comprehending psychosomatic conditions.

Charcot's charismatic lecture style captured widespread acclaim, drawing students, clinicians, and scholars globally to witness his compelling demonstrations. His mesmerizing presentations on hysteria and hypnosis not only captivated audiences but incited passionate debate within the medical community, heralding a new era of critical analysis and exploration in both neurology and psychiatry (Didi-Huberman, 2003; Lepoutre & Villa, 2015). Furthermore, Charcot's advocacy for interdisciplinary collaboration epitomized his progressive vision; he transcended disciplinary borders, fostering an environment rich in intellectual exchange. By promoting dialogue between neurologists, psychologists, and psychiatrists, he endeavored to cultivate a holistic appreciation of the mind-body relationship, profoundly influencing subsequent developments within psychology and psychiatry.

In summary, Jean-Martin Charcot's indelible influence on neurology and his pioneering contributions to the exploration of hysteria continue to echo within contemporary medical discourse. His relentless pursuit of scientific integrity, coupled with his profound impact on medical education and clinical practice, cements his stature as a trailblazing figure whose legacy perpetuates inspiration and guidance for both current and forthcoming generations of medical professionals (Mathon et al., 2018).

Charcot's Salpêtrière Hospital: The Epicenter of Hysteria Research

By the dawn of the 20th century, Salpêtrière Hospital in Paris emerged as a pivotal enclave for the study of hysteria under the influential guidance of Jean-Martin Charcot. Renowned for his pathbreaking work in neurology, Charcot transformed this institution into a seminal center for understanding and treating hysteria, a condition predominantly affecting women and shrouded in enigma (Esman, 2011). The establishment provided an unprecedented venue for an exhaustive exploration of hysteria in all its manifestations, drawing the attention of academics, physicians, and an inquisitive public alike.

At Salpêtrière, Charcot meticulously documented and analyzed a plethora of hysteria cases, employing a blend of clinical observations, experimental methodologies, and public exhibitions. Such efforts fostered a more profound understanding of the condition and laid the groundwork for innovative therapeutic approaches. Moreover, the hospital's diverse patient demographic facilitated an expansive research scope, enabling Charcot to discern various distinct patterns and idiosyncrasies within the spectrum of hysterical disorders (Lepoutre & Villa, 2015).

One particularly noteworthy aspect of Charcot's tenure was his incorporation of hypnosis as a diagnostic and therapeutic instrument in the examination of hysteria. Through dramatic public demonstrations, Charcot exhibited the induction of hysterical attacks and the subsequent control enacted through hypnotic techniques. These captivating showcases ensnared not only the medical community but also captivated the wider public, engendering a broader interest and discourse surrounding the enigmatic nature of hysteria (Bogousslavsky, 2011).

Consequently, the Salpêtrière Hospital became a central nexus for the convergence of medical, psychological, and sociocultural inquiries into hysteria. Scholars flocked to observe Charcot's sessions and to partake in rich academic discourse, triggering a significant shift in the perception and understanding of this condition. Furthermore, the hospital's influence radiated beyond academic confines, permeating artistic and literary domains, thereby shaping popular representations and narratives regarding hysteria in broader society (Yılmaz, 2021).

Charcot's efforts at Salpêtrière radically altered the contours of hysteria studies, establishing foundational groundwork for subsequent advancements in mental health. His meticulous investigations and innovative methodologies contributed not only to scientific progress but also illuminated the necessity for nuanced, compassionate approaches to deciphering and addressing complex psychological phenomena.

The Public Demonstrations: Hypnosis and Hysterical Episodes

In the late 19th century, Paris crystallized as the epicenter of revolutionary medical demonstrations at the Salpêtrière Hospital, orchestrated under the aegis of Jean-Martin Charcot. Charcot's implementation of hypnosis as a therapeutic modality for hysteria and his theatrical public demonstrations mesmerized audiences while advancing the comprehension of this elusive condition. These exhibitions served as a focal point for elucidating the manifestations of hysteria, engendering heightened interest and considerable controversy both within the medical realm and beyond (Cardeña & Nijenhuis, 2001).

During these demonstrations, Charcot would induce hypnotic states in patients—predominantly women diagnosed with hysteria—as a means of showcasing their multifarious symptoms and expressions. These episodes aimed to reveal the spectrum of hysterical attacks, encompassing paralysis, convulsions, and trance-like states. Charcot's thorough documentation of these displays significantly contributed to the scientific recognition and understanding of hysteria as a legitimate medical phenomenon (Freud, 2001; Sugarman, 2016).

His emphasis on the physiological dimensions of hysteria, coupled with the employment of hypnosis, challenged prevailing assumptions regarding the purely psychological etiology of the condition. Charcot's integrative approach underscored myths surrounding hysteria's nature, thereby opening novel avenues for investigation and dialogue within the burgeoning fields of neurology and psychology (Libbrecht & Quackelbeen, 1995). The social and cultural ramifications of these demonstrations were profound, instigating widespread speculation and fascination with hysteria while concurrently raising ethical queries about patient consent and the potential commodification of vulnerable individuals for scientific inquiry.

The dramatic tenor of these public exhibitions, accentuated by Charcot's authoritative presence and meticulous scrutiny, attracted considerable intrigue within professional circles and permeated popular culture. Charcot's charisma and theatrical flair during these presentations impacted not solely the medical community but also exerted influence upon contemporary artists and literary figures. The striking imagery and narratives emerging from these high-profile events significantly molded the representations of hysteria in literature, art, and drama, thereby perpetuating the mystique surrounding the condition (Didi-Huberman, 2003).

Nevertheless, despite the acclaim and enthusiasm accompanying these demonstrations, they spurred skepticism and criticism. Some members of the medical establishment questioned the generalizability of Charcot's conclusions and the potential for suggestion to influence the observed hysterical manifestations (Yılmaz, 2021). Moreover, the gendered lens through which hysteria was examined and studied faced scrutiny, considering that many showcased patients were women, eliciting concerns regarding the objectification and exploitation of female subjects.

The public demonstrations orchestrated by Charcot constitute a seminal moment in the historical evolution of hysteria, symbolizing a transition toward a more systematic and empirical exploration of the condition. The legacy of these events resonates profoundly through the chronicles of medical and cultural history, leaving an indelible imprint on the perception and investigation of hysteria and its myriad manifestations.

Freud Meets Charcot: The Embryonic Foundations of Psychoanalytic Thought

In the closing decades of the 19th century, the realms of neurology and psychology converged in an extraordinary alliance as Sigmund Freud, a young and aspiring physician, ventured into the intricate world of hysteria under the mentorship of Jean-Martin Charcot. This seminal encounter would forge the foundational pillars for the groundbreaking theory of psychoanalysis (Oliveira et al., 2018). As Freud immersed himself in Charcot's innovative methodologies at the Salpêtrière Hospital in Paris, he witnessed the puzzling manifestations of hysteria alongside Charcot's pioneering techniques, which sought to probe the depths of the human psyche (Freud, 2001).

Charcot's profound influence on Freud significantly shaped the latter's early comprehension of the complexities surrounding mental disorders. Through painstaking observation and collaboration, Freud assimilated Charcot's emphasis on the pivotal role that psychological factors play in the etiology of neuroses (Mathon et al., 2018). It was during this transformative period that the concepts of repression and psychic determinism—cornerstones of psychoanalytic theory—began to take root within Freud's burgeoning intellectual framework.

Moreover, it was Charcot's employment of hypnosis as a mechanism for excavating buried traumas that particularly captivated Freud, ultimately becoming integral to his therapeutic practices. Witnessing the remarkable recoveries of patients with hysterical presentations as they unspooled their past traumas through hypnotic suggestion illuminated Freud's path to exploring the intricacies of the unconscious mind (Esman, 2011). This exposure unveiled the repressed experiences that underpinned pathological conditions, thereby molding his theoretical perspective.

The synergy between Charcot's neurological acumen and Freud's emerging insights into the labyrinthine nature of the human psyche cultivated an environment rich in intellectual curiosity, catalyzing the genesis of psychoanalytic thought. Within this confluence of clinical experience and theoretical inquiry, Freud's theories on the unconscious, dream interpretation, and psychosexual development began to germinate, heralding a paradigm shift in the understanding and treatment of psychological disorders (Lepoutre & Villa, 2015).

The dialogue between Freud and Charcot not only elevated the discourse surrounding hysteria in medical and academic circles but also sowed the seeds for a transformative framework to comprehend human consciousness. The Charcot-Freud collaboration exemplified the profound impact of interdisciplinary engagement, birthing an innovative approach that transcended conventional medical paradigms and paved the way for the emergence of modern psychoanalysis as a distinct academic field.

Sigmund Freud's Early Work on Hysteria

As Freud navigated the late 19th century, he embarked on a journey that would indelibly impact psychology and radically alter our understanding of hysteria. His collaboration with Jean-Martin Charcot at Salpêtrière Hospital marked the genesis of his investigative endeavor into the esoteric nature of hysteria (Yılmaz, 2021). In his fervent pursuit of knowledge, Freud interrogated the prevailing paradigms related to the disorder's etiology and manifestations.

With relentless determination, he undertook extensive clinical observations, diligently documenting the varied symptoms and narratives shared by his patients experiencing hysteria. This meticulous groundwork not only became the foundation of his innovative theories but also paved the way for the development of contemporary psychoanalytic techniques (Freud, 2001). Freud's recognition of the substantial influence of early life experiences on the emergence of hysterical symptoms became one of his most significant contributions during this period.

He ardently emphasized the intricate interplay between repressed memories, unconscious conflicts, and the manifestation of hysterical symptoms. Unpacking these deeply held psychological elements became the centerpiece of Freud's therapeutic approach. Employing introspective dialogue and the progressive technique of free association, he skillfully unearthed the traumas and suppressed desires that interwove with his patients' hysterical presentations (Sugarman, 2016). This revolutionary method not only transformed the treatment of hysteria but also instigated a profound shift in the public perception of mental illness.

Freud's early work on hysteria encapsulated his unyielding quest for truth while delineating a trajectory for the evolution of psychoanalytic thought. His insatiable curiosity, coupled with a steadfast commitment to decode the complexities of the human psyche, culminated in a body of work that resonates within the canon of psychological inquiry (Micale, 1995). In essence, Freud's initial exploration of hysteria illuminated a pathway toward deeper comprehension of the intricate tapestry that constitutes the human mind, leaving profound implications for future psychological discourse.

From Hypnosis to Free Association: The Evolution of Freud's Techniques

As Freud delved deeper into the enigmatic domain of hysteria, his therapeutic methodology underwent a significant evolution, transitioning from hypnosis to free association. This shift represented a pivotal moment in the refinement of psychoanalytic techniques. Initially, Freud relied on hypnosis to access the unconscious mind and reveal repressed traumas and conflicts intrinsic to hysterical symptoms. However, he soon recognized the inherent limitations of this approach, noting that it often led to the suppression or distortion of pivotal aspects within the patient's psyche (Yılmaz, 2021).

Freud's disenchantment with hypnosis ultimately catalyzed the innovation of free association—a revolutionary technique encouraging patients to express their unfiltered thoughts and emotions without censorship or restraint. By permitting the unconscious to surface unimpeded, Freud believed individuals could gradually unveil the deep-seated origins of their psychological distress, gaining invaluable insights into their inner workings (Freud, 2001). Free association opened pathways for exploring dreams, memories, and fantasies, enriching Freud's emerging theories regarding the complexities of the human psyche.

This transition away from hypnosis was accompanied by a profound reconceptualization of the therapist's role. Rather than asserting an authoritative stance during hypnosis, Freud adopted a more passive and observational approach, emphasizing neutrality and non-directiveness. This strategic pivot established the fundamental principles of psychoanalysis, cultivating a dynamic interplay between the analyst and the analysand that fostered an environment conducive to introspection and self-discovery.

Furthermore, the introduction of free association heralded a paradigm shift in the understanding of psychopathology. Freud's focus on the significance of seemingly trivial details, linguistic slips, and disjointed thoughts propelled the exploration of the unconscious to the vanguard of psychological inquiry. The intricate layers of an individual's psyche were no longer perceived as an impenetrable enigma but rather as a mosaic awaiting interpretation through nuanced exploration of associations and meanings (Cardeña & Nijenhuis, 2001).

In essence, the transition from hypnosis to free association encapsulated Freud's relentless ambition to construct a comprehensive framework for unraveling the enigmas of hysteria and other manifestations of mental anguish. This transformative progression not only revolutionized therapeutic methodologies but also heralded a seismic shift in the understanding of human psychology, laying the groundwork for the enduring legacy of psychoanalysis.

The Birth of Psychoanalysis: Hysteria as a Gateway

During the late 19th century, hysteria emerged as a key catalyst in the nascent development of psychoanalysis, radically reshaping the landscape of psychology and redefining the understanding of mental illness. This pivotal era witnessed the convergence of the groundbreaking efforts of Jean-Martin Charcot and Sigmund Freud, resulting in the formulation of psychoanalytic theory and practice. Hysteria, characterized by its multifaceted manifestations and elusive qualities, served as fertile ground for Freud's innovative inquiries into the human psyche (Libbrecht & Quackelbeen, 1995).

Central to this exploration was the recognition that hysteria transcended mere eccentric symptoms; it was a manifestation of unconscious psychological processes and repressed memories. This realization signified the dawn of a new era in mental health care. Freud's pioneering methodology involved probing the depths of the patient's subconscious through techniques such as dream analysis, free association, and the interpretation of lapses of language (Bogousslavsky, 2011; Sugarman, 2016). These methods sought to reveal the root causes of neurotic symptoms, disentangling the complex web of unconscious conflicts and desires that lay beneath the surface.

Hysteria, with its myriad physical and emotional expressions, provided Freud with a canvas to illustrate his revolutionary theories on the mind. The concept of transference, wherein patients projected their unconscious emotions onto their therapist, elucidated the intricate dynamics interwoven within the phenomena of hysteria and neurosis. As Freud elucidated the latent meanings underpinning seemingly irrational behaviors and symptoms, the framework of psychoanalysis began to coalesce, offering profound insights into the human psyche.

Beyond its theoretical ramifications, the study of hysteria and its corresponding treatment established the therapeutic relationship as a central tenet of psychoanalysis. Through empathic understanding and a nonjudgmental stance, therapists could navigate the complex terrain of a patient's internal world, cultivating a safe haven for the exploration of deeply embedded emotions and experiences (Micale, 1995). This transformative approach, rooted in the rich legacy of hysteria, continues to inform modern psychotherapeutic practices, underscoring the enduring significance of hysteria as a gateway to profound psychoanalytic insights.

Influence of Charcot and Freud on Later Psychopathology

The substantial contributions of Jean-Martin Charcot and Sigmund Freud to the study of psychopathology resonate throughout contemporary psychology. Charcot's foundational work in neurology, particularly at the Salpêtrière Hospital, established a critical framework for understanding various psychiatric disorders. His rigorous emphasis on empirical observation and meticulous documentation set a precedent for future research and clinical practice, fostering a detailed approach to diagnosing and treating mental illnesses (Mathon et al., 2018). In addition, Charcot's captivating demonstrations of hysteria and hypnosis not only engaged the medical community but also spurred an intensified interest in the investigation of psychological phenomena and altered states of consciousness (Esman, 2011).

Freud, deeply influenced by Charcot's pioneering methods, adopted and expanded upon many of his foundational ideas. Through his early investigations into hysteria, Freud formulated groundbreaking theories that revolutionized the landscape of psychopathology. The concept of the unconscious mind, which Freud synthesized from his observations of patients suffering from hysteria, became a cornerstone of psychoanalytic theory, fundamentally reshaping the understanding of mental disorders (Yılmaz, 2021). Furthermore, Freud's establishment of psychoanalysis as a therapeutic modality marked a paradigm shift in the treatment of psychological conditions, ushering in a new era of talk therapy and introspective exploration.

The enduring impact of Charcot and Freud permeates contemporary psychopathology in myriad ways. Their focus on the subconscious, repressed memories, and early childhood experiences paved the way for a nuanced understanding of the complex interplay between psyche, behavior, and pathology (Bogousslavsky,

2020). Many modern therapeutic methodologies draw inspiration from Freud's psychoanalytic innovations, employing techniques such as dream interpretation, transference, and free association to uncover unconscious conflicts and facilitate healing.

Moreover, the legacies of Charcot and Freud are evident in the evolution of diagnostic categories and the understanding of mental health disorders. Their pioneering efforts ignited further scientific inquiry into the nature of psychological distress, leading to the formulation of comprehensive diagnostic criteria and a more sophisticated grasp of conditions previously shrouded in obscurity (Didi-Huberman, 2003). The recognition of trauma, dissociation, and somatization as integral components of many psychiatric disorders owe much to the foundational work laid by Charcot and Freud, underscoring their lasting influence on the field of psychopathology.

Legacy and Critique: Reevaluating 19th Century Contributions

As we reflect on Charcot and Freud's profound impact on the understanding of psychopathology, it is imperative to evaluate their enduring legacy. Both figures transformed not only the psychiatric profession but also societal perceptions of mental illness, particularly concerning hysteria. Their work laid the groundwork for subsequent advancements in psychology, significantly shaping how clinicians approached and conceptualized mental disorders (Libbrecht & Quackelbeen, 1995).

Charcot's focus on the anatomical and neurological underpinnings of hysteria heralded a paradigm shift in the understanding of psychological disturbances, challenging existing beliefs that linked these conditions solely to moral failings or character flaws. His influential demonstrations at Salpêtrière Hospital undoubtedly contributed to the burgeoning fields of neurology and psychiatry, effectively legitimizing the study of hysteria and serving as a model for later diagnostic practices (Bogousslavsky, 2011).

In contrast, Freud's pioneering development of psychoanalysis propelled an in-depth exploration of unconscious motivations and repressed desires—an approach that significantly influenced subsequent theories of psychopathology. His innovative techniques, including free association and dream analysis, unlocked new pathways for understanding the complexities of human behavior and the intricacies of mental suffering (Sugarman, 2016). The enduring legacy of his work is evidenced by the continued relevance of psychoanalytic principles within contemporary therapeutic practices.

Despite their monumental contributions, the 19th-century views of Charcot and Freud have not evaded critique. Modern scholars have scrutinized their approaches, acknowledging both the groundbreaking insights they offered and the constraints imposed by their cultural contexts. Criticisms encompass issues of gender bias, Eurocentrism, and the ethical challenges stemming from the utilization of vulnerable patients in clinical demonstrations (Smith-Rosenberg, 2016).

Moreover, the very notion of hysteria has been reevaluated and redefined within the broader framework of mental health. Contemporary assessments seek to acknowledge the diversity and complexity of human experiences while addressing the historical pathologization of emotions, particularly those correlated with women. By revisiting and critiquing the legacies of Charcot and Freud, we engage in a vital dialogue about the evolution of psychiatric thought and the ongoing pursuit of a more inclusive and compassionate approach to understanding and treating mental distress.

In a Nutshell:

The 19th Century Breakthroughs: Charcot, Freud, and Psychopathology

The 19th century was a pivotal period for the development of modern psychopathology, with significant contributions from Jean-Martin Charcot and Sigmund Freud. Charcot, often regarded as the father of modern neurology, had a profound influence on Freud, who later founded psychoanalysis. This synthesis explores the key insights from various research papers on the relationship between Charcot, Freud, and the evolution of psychopathology.

Key Insights

- **Charcot's Influence on Freud's Career and Psychoanalytic Theory:**

  - Charcot's teachings at the Salpêtrière Hospital significantly influenced Freud, shifting his focus from general neurology to the study of hysteria, hypnosis, and psychological issues, which laid the groundwork for psychoanalytic theory.

- **Diagnostic Preoccupation and Nosological Method:**

  - Freud's attention to diagnostic distinctions and his development of a nosological system were heavily influenced by Charcot's diagnostic methods. This focus on diagnosis was a crucial orga-

nizing principle in Freud's early writings and the
development of psychoanalysis.

- **Hysteria and Hypnosis**:

  ○ Charcot's work on hysteria, including the role of
    trauma and environmental influences, was foun-
    dational for Freud. Charcot's use of hypnosis to
    treat hysteria also inspired Freud to explore and
    eventually develop psychoanalytic techniques.

- **Male Hysteria and Psychical Trauma**:

  ○ Charcot's identification of male hysteria and the
    concept of traumatic hysteria influenced Freud's
    early theories on psychical trauma. Freud's notion
    that each hysterical symptom is due to a psychical
    trauma reviving an earlier traumatic event was de-
    veloped in reference to Charcot's ideas.

- **Shift from Neurology to Psychopathology**:

  ○ Freud's transition from neurology to psy-
    chopathology was marked by his exposure to
    Charcot's clinical-descriptive method, which em-
    phasized clinical observations over anatomical in-
    vestigations. This shift was crucial for the foun-
    dation of psychoanalysis.

- **Role of Sexuality in Psychopathology**:

  ○ Charcot's insights into the role of sexual factors in
    hysteria influenced Freud's lifelong conviction of
    the central role of sexuality and sexual repression
    in the etiology of neuroses.

Conclusion

The relationship between Jean-Martin Charcot and Sigmund Freud was instrumental in the development of modern psychopathology. Charcot's influence on Freud extended from diagnostic methods to the study of hysteria and the use of hypnosis, ultimately leading to the foundation of psychoanalysis. Freud's shift from neurology to psychopathology and his focus on the role of trauma and sexuality in mental disorders were deeply rooted in Charcot's teachings. This synthesis highlights the profound impact of Charcot on Freud's career and the evolution of psychopathology in the 19th century.

References

Bogousslavsky, J. (2011). Sigmund Freud's evolution from neurology to psychiatry. Neurology, 77, 1391-1394. https://doi.org/10.1212/WNL.0b013e31823152a1

Bogousslavsky, J. (2020). The mysteries of hysteria: a historical perspective. International Review of Psychiatry, 32, 437-450. https://doi.org/10.1080/09540261.2020.1772731

Cardeña, E., & Nijenhuis, E. (2001). Embodied Sorrow. Journal of Trauma & Dissociation, 1, 1-5. https://doi.org/10.1300/J229v01n04_01

Didi-Huberman, G. (2003). Invention of Hysteria: Charcot and the Photographic Iconography of the Salpêtrière. MIT Press.

Esman, A. (2011). Charcot, Freud, and the treatment of "nervous disorders". The Journal of nervous and mental disease, 199(11), 828-829. https://doi.org/10.1097/NMD.0b013e3182348cf9

Freud, S. (2001). Studies on hysteria (J. Strachey, Trans.). Basic Books.

Lepoutre, T., & Villa, F. (2015). Freud with Charcot: Freud's discovery and the question of diagnosis. The International Journal of Psychoanalysis, 96, 345-368. https://doi.org/10.1111/1745-8315.12247

Libbrecht, K., & Quackelbeen, J. (1995). On the early history of male hysteria and psychic trauma. Charcot's influence on Freudian thought. Journal of the history of the behavioral sciences, 31(4), 370-384.

Mathon, B., Amelot, A., Clemenceau, S., Carpentier, A., & Boch, A. (2018). Commentary: La Pitié-Salpêtrière Hospital in Paris: the Historic Cradle of Neurosurgery. Neurosurgery, 82, 164–174.

Micale, M. S. (1995). Approaching hysteria: Disease and its interpretations. Princeton University Press.

Oliveira, L., Teive, H., Marques, P., Germiniani, F., & Paola, L. (2018). Jean-Martin Charcot's influence on Sigmund Freud's career (P5.309). Neurology. https://doi.org/10.1212/wnl.90.15 _supplement.p5.309

Smith-Rosenberg, C. (2016). THE HYSTERICAL WOMAN: SEX ROLES AND ROLE CONFLICT IN 19th-CENTURY AMERICA. https://doi.org/10.1515/9783110976328.101

Sugarman, S. (2016). Freud on psychoanalysis: Five Lectures on Psychoanalysis (1909a), 4-14. https://doi.org/10.1017/CBO978 1316340240.002

Yılmaz, Y. (2021). Freud's Encounter with Charcot and His Epistemological Break. Uluslararası Sosyal Bilimler Akademi Dergisi. https://doi.org/10.47994/USBAD.896740

CHAPTER FIVE

SYMPTOMATOLOGY OF HYSTERIA: DEFINING THE INDEFINABLE

The Historical Evolution of Hysteria Symptoms

Hysteria, an intellectually provocative condition typified by an extensive range of manifestations, has long captivated historians, medical practitioners, and cultural commentators alike. The ancients, particularly the Greeks, postulated that it was a disorder borne of a mobile uterus, hence the etymological roots of the term 'hysteria,' derived from the Greek word for uterus (Bustos et al., 2014). This conjecture initiated a prolonged phase of misconceptions and misapprehensions surrounding the disorder, rippling through centuries. During the Middle Ages and the Renaissance, hysteria was often perceived through the lens of demonic possession or witchcraft, with symptomatic expressions interpreted as manifestations of supernatural forces (Chodoff, 1974).

As medical science progressed, fresh paradigms regarding hysteria came to the forefront. The 19th century marked a pivotal junc-

ture with the contributions of neurologist Jean-Martin Charcot
and psychologist Sigmund Freud. Charcot's investigations illuminated the physical manifestations of hysteria—encompassing phenomena like paralysis and seizures—while Freud ventured into the
labyrinthine psychological dimensions, positing that unconscious
conflicts were crucial in the genesis of such symptoms (Marsden,
1986; Miller, 1988). These disparate interpretations catalyzed divergent methodologies in identifying and treating hysteria (Munts
& Koehler, 2010).

The mind-body nexus has been central to the historical conception of hysterical symptoms. Physicians and philosophers engaged
in fervent debates about whether the manifestations were purely
physiological or deeply entrenched in psychological disturbances
(Parr, 1959). This ongoing dialogue not only shaped perceptions
of hysteria but also significantly influenced therapeutic approaches.

Over time, sociocultural perceptions and prevailing norms have
further colored the representation and interpretation of hysteria
symptoms. For instance, during tumultuous periods, such as wars
or social upheavals, there was often a discernible rise in hysteria-like
cases, suggesting a profound interplay between external stressors
and symptomatology (Kimble et al., 1975). Gender biases and
stereotypes have further obfuscated the understanding of hysterical symptoms, resulting in inequitable diagnostic criteria for men
versus women (Mancini et al., 2022).

The historical framing of hysteria not only chronicles the trajectory of medical knowledge but also reflects broader societal attitudes toward mental health and emotional expression, revealing
a complex interplay of factors that have shaped this enigmatic
condition.

Somatic Manifestations: The Body in Distress

The somatic expressions of hysteria have intrigued and perplexed scholarly circles for centuries. In antiquity, physicians ascribed a plethora of physical symptoms to the wandering womb, epitomizing a long-standing belief in the female body's inherent vulnerability to hysteria (Foucault, 1980). These manifestations range from convulsions and paralysis to aphonia and sensory abnormalities, underscoring the intricate interrelationship between psychological turmoil and corporeal expression (Sacks, 2012).

From the medieval epoch to contemporary times, the somatic symptoms associated with hysteria have morphed, reflecting evolving societal understandings and medical interpretations of this multifaceted disorder. Grappling with the complexities of these bodily expressions is vital for unraveling the profound effects of hysteria on both individuals and society at large. The embodiment of hysteria through these somatic manifestations often narrates a heartrending tale of distress and marginalization, illustrating the intersection of internal disquiet and external realities, whereby the body becomes a canvas for the articulation of emotional and psychological agony (Perley & Guze, 1962).

Moreover, the somatic features of hysteria confront traditional binaries separating mind and body, beckoning recognition of their interdependence. Through a thorough examination of these manifestations, we glean insights into the somber ramifications of psychological distress that remains unaddressed or misinterpreted (Reed, 1975). Additionally, this discourse invites scrutiny into the sociocultural influences shaping the presentation and interpretation of bodily symptoms, illuminating the roles of gender, socioeconomic status, and cultural milieu in the experience of illness.

As we navigate this intricate tapestry of somatic expressions, we engage with the compelling, yet elusive essence of hysteria, appreciating the lasting effects of its diverse manifestations on the lives of those afflicted.

Psychological Expressions: The Mind Unveiled

The inquiry into the psychological expressions of hysteria delves into the labyrinthine terrain of the human psyche, where manifestations of distress and anxiety often reveal their most intricate forms. Venturing beyond the palpable somatic symptoms, this aspect of hysteria transcends the corporeal realm, unveiling the subtleties and profundities of psychological turmoil (Celani & C., 1976). The manifestations of hysteria provide an aperture into the depths of the human subconscious, capturing the interest of scholars, clinicians, and society throughout the ages.

At the heart of this exploration lies the endeavor to unravel the subconscious motivations and emotional currents that surface in bewildering forms. From perplexing paralysis to dramatic emotional eruptions, these symptoms serve as a mirror reflecting the complexities residing within the human mind. The historical chronicles of hysterical psychological expressions intertwine with societal expectations, gender dynamics, and the nexus between individual experiences and overarching cultural influences (Miller, 1988).

The shifting diagnostic criteria over time have further sculpted our comprehension of psychological manifestations associated with hysteria. The discerning insight of psychiatrists and psychologists throughout history has sought to illuminate these enigmatic expressions, evolving from the ancient notion of a wandering womb to contemporary psychiatric classification systems (Foucault, 1980). This intellectual journey allows us to trace the development of our understanding of psychological expressions tied to hysteria, revealing the intricate interplay between societal perceptions and personal experiences.

Contemporary research continues to illuminate the intricate network of psychological expressions associated with hysteria, providing valuable insights into the underlying mechanisms that generate these multifarious symptoms (Mancini et al., 2022). This knowledge not only fosters empathy and affirmation for individuals experiencing such phenomena but also facilitates the emergence of more nuanced diagnostic and therapeutic approaches, aiming to eradicate stigma.

Exploring these unveiled psychological expressions within the context of hysteria compels contemplation of the complexities of human consciousness, the delicate interplay between psyche and soma, and the substantial implications for individual welfare and societal perspectives on mental health.

Diagnostic Criteria Through the Ages

The diagnostic frameworks for hysteria have markedly evolved, influenced by shifting societal beliefs, medical paradigms, and cultural narratives (Bustos et al., 2014). Early civilizations, including the Egyptians and Greeks, attributed hysterical symptoms to a wandering womb, resulting in rudimentary and often deleterious treatment modalities. In medieval Europe, hysteria was viewed through the lens of demonic possession, prompting practices such as exorcisms and other religious interventions (Chodoff, 1974). The Renaissance heralded a transition towards a more medicalized understanding, with practitioners striving to classify and diagnose hysteria based on observable symptoms, albeit without systematic rigor and heavily laden with superstitions and gender biases.

The dawn of modern medicine in the 19th century precipitated significant strides in comprehending hysteria and other mental health maladies. Pioneering figures such as Jean-Martin Charcot and Sigmund Freud were instrumental in shaping the diagnostic criteria for hysteria. Charcot's pivotal work at the Salpêtrière Hospital introduced the notion of 'hysterical attacks,' underscoring the importance of clinical observation (Marsden, 1986). Freud's psychoanalytic theories posited that hysterical symptoms were often manifestations of repressed psychological conflicts, laying the groundwork for subsequent psychiatric evaluations (Miller, 1988).

As psychiatry burgeoned, the diagnostic criteria for hysteria underwent continual refinement. Its inclusion in early editions of the Diagnostic and Statistical Manual of Mental Disorders (DSM) mirrored evolving perspectives on mental health classifications (Perley & Guze, 1962). However, the term hysteria became increasingly contentious due to its historical links with sexism and the medicalization of women's emotions, ultimately leading to its removal from more recent iterations of the DSM and highlighting the intricate interplay among medical knowledge, societal norms, and gender politics.

In contemporary practice, the diagnostic frameworks for hysteria have predominantly transitioned to more inclusive classifications like somatic symptom disorders and conversion disorder (Munts & Koehler, 2010). These advanced paradigms strive to encapsulate both psychological and somatic dimensions of distress, all while minimizing stigma and gender bias. Understanding the historical evolution of diagnostic criteria furnishes profound insights into the enduring impact of cultural norms and scientific advancements on the conceptualization of mental health disorders.

The Influence of Societal Contexts on Symptom Presentation

The expression of symptoms associated with hysteria has been perpetually molded by the societal contexts in which individuals reside, sculpting how these symptoms are perceived and represented

(Foucault, 1980). Throughout history, prevailing norms, values, and beliefs have significantly swayed the presentation and interpretation of hysterical symptoms. In eras characterized by rigid gender roles, women, in particular, faced stringent behavioral expectations; deviations from these norms were often pathologized as signs of hysteria. In cultures where emotional expressions are stigmatized or curtailed, the psychological dimensions of hysteria may be expressed in atypical ways, leading to misinterpretation or neglect (Mancini et al., 2022).

The ramifications of societal expectations extend beyond individual experiences, impacting diagnostic frameworks and therapeutic interventions. Prevailing attitudes have historically delineated the parameters of acceptable behavior, indelibly shaping medical understandings of what constitutes 'abnormal' symptom presentation (Reed, 1975). Moreover, social perceptions related to race, class, and gender have historically played a significant role in the interpretation of symptoms, especially for marginalized groups, who often face additional barriers to validation and understanding of their experiences (Celani & C., 1976).

Grasping the influence of sociocultural contexts on symptom presentation is pivotal for cultivating comprehensive and culturally attuned diagnostic and therapeutic approaches. It necessitates an exhaustive examination of the interplay between individual experiences and broader sociopolitical dynamics, aiming to dismantle the biases and stereotypes that may obstruct accurate comprehension and support for individuals manifesting hysterical symptoms.

A profound awareness of these societal determinants informs healthcare professionals, enabling them to navigate the complexities of diagnosis and tailor interventions to the unique needs of each patient effectively (Kimble et al., 1975). By acknowledging the multifaceted societal influences on symptom presentation, we can aspire to create a more equitable and inclusive healthcare system that recognizes the intricate nature of human experiences.

Gender Differences in Symptomatology

Gender differentials significantly influence the manifestation and interpretation of hysterical symptoms, entrenched as they are in historical and sociocultural dynamics. Throughout the ages, the perception of hysteria has often been viewed through a gendered lens, with a discernible bias leading to the attribution of symptoms predominantly to women (Mancini et al., 2022). These biases have notably molded the understanding and diagnostic criteria for hysteria, resulting in a plethora of misconceptions (Celani & C., 1976). Furthermore, the societal expectations and pressures imposed on women have invariably contributed to the emergence and expression of hysterical symptoms.

Gender-specific stressors—including the realities of motherhood, reproductive health challenges, and socioeconomic disparities—can markedly affect how hysteria presents itself in women (Perley & Guze, 1962). The historical tendency to pathologize female emotions and behaviors perpetuates the notion that women are inherently more susceptible to developing hysterical reactions. Consequently, the intertwining of biological, psychological, and sociocultural elements has engendered distinct patterns of symptomatology divergent across the genders. Empirical studies often indicate that women are more likely to present somatic complaints, such as pain syndromes, gastrointestinal disturbances, and convulsions, whereas men may predominantly exhibit psychological manifestations, including dissociative symptoms and altered states of consciousness (Miller, 1988).

Acknowledging these gender discrepancies is crucial for ensuring accurate, fair diagnoses and equitable treatment protocols. Exploring the gendered dimensions of hysteria further enriches our understanding of the complex interplay between biological, psychological, and social determinants in health. By recognizing these gender-specific subtleties, practitioners can adopt more inclusive and comprehensive strategies to manage and support individuals grappling with hysterical symptoms, moving beyond entrenched stereotypes and biases (Chodoff, 1974).

The Role of Stress and Trauma in Symptom Development

Stress and trauma serve as critical catalysts in the genesis and manifestation of hysteria-related symptoms (Munts & Koehler, 2010). Both historical texts and contemporary research unmistakably underscore the impact of adverse life experiences on an individual's mental and physical health. Investigating the intricate nexus between stress, trauma, and hysteria reveals invaluable insights into the multifaceted nature of symptom development.

Individuals entrenched in prolonged or intense stress may exhibit a plethora of symptoms characteristic of hysteria, ranging from inexplicable physical ailments like paralysis and seizures to emotional and cognitive disturbances such as dissociation, amnesia, anxiety, and depression (Perley & Guze, 1962). Traumatic experiences—be they instances of physical or emotional abuse, accidents, or exposure to combat situations—often act as precipitating factors for the onset of hysterical symptoms. The relationship between stress, trauma, and hysteria is inherently intricate, with the mind and body executing responses that frequently defy conventional comprehension.

For instance, conversion disorder exemplifies how psychological anguish can materialize as physical ailments, emphasizing the complex interplay between emotional turmoil and physiological reactions (Miller, 1988). Furthermore, individuals with a history of trauma are statistically at a greater risk for developing both somatic and psychological symptoms reminiscent of those associated with hysteria. The enduring impact of past traumatic events illustrates their persistent influence on an individual's holistic well-being, spotlighting the complexities enveloping symptom development in hysteria.

Recognizing the profound effects of stress and trauma on symptomology is essential for advocating holistic treatment approaches for individuals exhibiting hysterical manifestations. By acknowledging the roles of these factors, healthcare providers, caregivers, and society at large can engender a more empathetic, nuanced understanding of hysteria and its ramifications. This deeper comprehension fosters pathways to improved care, validation, and therapeutic interventions tailored specifically to address the unique needs of those navigating the intricate landscape of hysterical symptoms inspired by stress and trauma.

Misinterpretations and Myths Surrounding Hysterical Symptoms

Hysteria has historically been shrouded in a fog of misinterpretations and myths, with these misconceptions often leading to stigma and flawed beliefs about the intricacies of this complex condition (Miller, 1988). A pervasive myth suggests that hysteria manifests solely as a female disorder, neglecting to acknowledge that men can also endure similar symptomatology (Kimble et al., 1975). This gender-biased interpretation has further perpetuated societal inequities in the understanding and treatment of hysteria.

Additionally, the historical conflation of hysteria with supernatural or mystical forces has fostered a misleading belief in the inexplicability and untreatability of its symptoms, thus reinforcing the disorder's enigmatic reputation. Such misinterpretations have impeded scientific progress and sustained damaging stereotypes (Bustos et al., 2014). For example, the notion that hysteria represents mere attention-seeking behavior or malingering has cultivated dismissive attitudes from both medical practitioners and the general populace towards individuals genuinely suffering from identifiable symptoms.

Another widespread myth posits that hysterical symptoms are exclusively psychogenic, devoid of any physiological underpinnings (Chodoff, 1974). This misconception commoditizes the intricate relationship between mental and bodily health and obstructs comprehensive methodologies aimed at addressing the diverse manifestations of hysteria. Historical misunderstandings surrounding the contagiousness of hysteria—often illustrated in accounts like the Salem witch trials—have additionally fueled fears and ostracized individuals exhibiting symptoms (Marsden, 1986).

The continued perpetuation of these myths has not only isolated affected individuals but has also obstructed accurate diagnosis and effective treatment protocols. Addressing and dismantling these pervasive misinterpretations is imperative for fostering a more informed and compassionate approach to hysteria. By debunking these fallacies, we can champion a greater understanding and support system for individuals grappling with the complexities of hysterical symptoms. It is critical for current discussions surrounding hysteria to confront and eliminate these myths, nurturing a more holistic and inclusive understanding of this intricate condition.

Symptom Evolution with Medical Advancements

The evolution of hysterical symptomatology in conjunction with medical advancements reveals a compelling narrative that reflects the shifting paradigms within psychiatric understanding and therapeutic methodologies. Historically, hysteria has endured various interpretations and diagnostic classifications, often resulting in the stigmatization of afflicted individuals (Celani & C., 1976). However, progress in medical science and the refinement of diagnostic instruments have fundamentally transformed our perceptions of hysteria and its associated symptoms (Foucault, 1980).

Early medical treatments for hysteria were primarily predicated on ideas such as the "wandering womb" and other somatic disturbances, leading to interventions that were often invasive and detrimental (Miller, 1988). As progress was made in neurobiology and psychology, the focus shifted toward recognizing the intricate interplay between emotional strife and physical manifestations (Munts & Koehler, 2010). The advent of psychoanalysis, bolstered by the contributions of pioneers like Sigmund Freud and Jean-Martin Charcot, facilitated a paradigm shift from viewing hysteria purely as a physical ailment to understanding it as deeply intertwined with psychological trauma (Marsden, 1986).

The introduction of standardized diagnostic criteria, such as those codified in the Diagnostic and Statistical Manual of Mental Disorders (DSM), has empowered clinicians to identify and characterize hysteria and related disorders more precisely (Perley & Guze, 1962). This delineation of specific symptom clusters and differentiation from other psychiatric conditions has illuminated what was once an enigmatic presentation.

Advancements in neuroimaging and psychophysiological assessments have yielded critical insights into the neural correlates accompanying hysteria symptoms. Such scientific breakthroughs have dispelled many myths and misconceptions surrounding the disorder, paving the way for more empathetic, evidence-based patient care (Kimble et al., 1975). Furthermore, the development of targeted psychotherapeutic interventions and pharmacological treatments tailored to the nuanced symptomatology of hysteria has markedly improved outcomes and quality of life for affected individuals.

Importantly, the evolution of hysterical symptoms does not solely hinge on medical advancements; it also mirrors broader societal changes. The increasing destigmatization of mental health concerns and the emphasis on holistic well-being have reshaped the discourse surrounding hysteria, inviting a more comprehensive and empathetic understanding of the condition (Mantsini et al., 2022).

In summation, the evolution of hysteria symptomatology through medical advancements showcases the dynamic nature of psychiatric knowledge and practice. As the intricate complexities of this condition continue to unfold, it remains essential to integrate the latest scientific findings with a compassionate, patient-centered approach, ensuring that individuals contending with hysterical symptoms receive the support and care they merit.

Modern Perspectives on Hysteria Symptomatology

In contemporary society, the understanding of hysteria symptomatology has significantly evolved. A more inclusive and multidimensional approach to mental health has catalyzed a fundamental reevaluation of how symptoms historically associated with hysteria are perceived and contextualized (Miller, 1988). Modern perspectives underscore the nuanced nature of these symptoms, recognizing their potential variability across individuals and cultural settings.

A hallmark of modern views on hysteria symptomatology is the emphasis on the interplay between biological, psychological, and social influences in shaping symptomatology. This holistic approach transcends reductionist frameworks of the past, appreciating the complexity of human experiences. Clinicians and researchers now increasingly recognize the need to consider the effects of trauma, stress, and sociocultural dynamics on symptom development and expression (Munts & Koehler, 2010). They acknowledge that manifestations once labeled 'hysterical' may, in fact, signify underlying trauma, somatic conditions, or genuine psychological conflict.

Moreover, contemporary frameworks prioritize the destigma-tization of traditionally hysterical symptoms. Instead of categor-ically dismissing these symptoms as exaggerated or invalid, there is a concerted effort to validate and understand them within the parameters of individual lived experiences and broader societal contexts (Mancini et al., 2022). An integral aspect of this shift in-cludes an increasing acknowledgment of the diversity of symptom manifestations among different demographic segments, encom-passing gender, ethnicity, and socioeconomic status.

Modern research further elucidates the intricate mind-body connection that underlies symptom expression, recognizing how emotional and psychological stress can present physically (Sacks, 2012). Such understanding is crucial for providing comprehensive and effective care to individuals presenting with symptoms that echo historical constructs of hysteria.

Additionally, technological advancements have greatly en-hanced our modern grasp of hysteria symptomatology. Neu-roimaging techniques, genetic explorations, and psychophysiolog-ical assessments have shed light on the underlying mechanisms facilitating symptom emergence, illuminating the neurobiological and genetic foundations of certain presentations (Miller, 1988). These developments have contributed to demystifying the enig-matic characteristics of hysteria symptoms and promoting more precise, individualized approaches to diagnosis and treatment.

In essence, modern perspectives on hysteria symptomatology represent a paradigm shift from stigmatizing and pathologizing symptoms towards embracing their complexity and recognizing the multifaceted nature of human suffering. By weaving together diverse disciplines and viewpoints, contemporary approaches en-deavor to deliver compassionate, evidence-based care that respects the autonomy and dignity of individuals experiencing symptoms historically associated with hysteria.

In a Nutshell:

Symptomatology of Hysteria: Defining the Indefinable

Hysteria, historically known as a complex and often controversial diagnosis, is characterized by symptoms that mimic physical or psychiatric disorders without an identifiable organic cause. This synthesis aims to consolidate the key insights from recent research papers on the symptomatology of hysteria.

Key Insights

- **Lack of Conventional Pathology**: Hysterical symptoms often present as indications of an underlying pathological process, yet no conventional pathology can be identified. Examples include sensory impairments that do not align with recognized anatomical distributions, suggesting the sensory system functions better than the symptoms indicate.

- **Secondary Gain and 'La Belle Indifference'**: Secondary gain (benefits derived from being ill) and 'la belle indifference' (a lack of concern about the symptoms) are traditionally associated with hysteria but are considered unreliable criteria. Secondary gain is common in many illnesses, and evidence suggests that general anxiety levels are often raised in patients with conversion hysteria, contradicting the notion of indifference.

- **Subjective Reality of Symptoms**: A central criterion for hysteria is that patients experience their symptoms as real and are not consciously aware of their
  non-pathological origins. This distinguishes hysteria
  from malingering, where symptoms are consciously
  simulated. However, this criterion is problematic as
  it requires subjective judgment about the patient's
  awareness, which is inherently unreliable.

- **Diagnostic Challenges**: In a clinical study of 120
  inpatients diagnosed with hysteria, only 13% exhibited purely hysterical symptoms. The rest had either
  a combination of hysterical and affective symptoms,
  only affective symptoms, or other uncertain diagnoses. This highlights the diagnostic challenges and
  the potential overlap with other conditions.

Conclusion

Hysteria is characterized by symptoms that lack a conventional pathological basis, often presenting sensory impairments or other physical symptoms that do not align with
known medical conditions. Traditional criteria like secondary
gain and 'la belle indifference' are unreliable, and the subjective reality of symptoms poses diagnostic challenges. The
overlap with other affective disorders further complicates the
diagnosis, underscoring the need for careful clinical evaluation.

References

Bustos, E., Galli, S., Haffen, E., & Moulin, T. (2014). Clinical manifestations of hysteria: an epistemological perspective or how historical dynamics illuminate current practice.. Frontiers of neurology and neuroscience, 35, 28-43. https://doi.org/10 .1159/000360436.

Celani, D., & , C. (1976). An interpersonal approach to hysteria.. The American journal of psychiatry, 133 12, 1414-8 . https://doi.org/10.1176/AJP.133.12.1414.

Chodoff, P. (1974). The diagnosis of hysteria: an overview. The American journal of psychiatry, 131 10, 1073-8. https://doi.org/10.1176/AJP.131.10.1073.

Foucault, M. (1980). The birth of the clinic: An archeology of medical perception. Vintage Books.

Kimble, R., Williams, J., & Agras, S. (1975). A comparison of two methods of diagnosing hysteria.. The American journal of psychiatry, 132 11, 1197-9. https://doi.org/10.1176/AJP.1 32.11.1197

Mancini, M., Scudiero, M., Mignogna, S., Urso, V., & Stanghellini, G. (2022). Se-duction is not sex-duction: Desexualizing and de-feminizing hysteria. Frontiers in Psychology, 13. https://doi.org/10.3389/fpsyg.2022.963117.

Marsden, C. (1986). Hysteria — a neurologist's view. Psychological Medicine, 16, 277 - 288. https://doi.org/10.1017/ S0033291700009090.

Miller, E. (1988). Defining hysterical symptoms. Psychological Medicine, 18, 275 - 277. https://doi.org/10.1017/S0033 291700007820.

Munts, A., & Koehler, P. (2010). How psychogenic is dystonia? Views from past to present. Brain : A Journal of Neurology, 133 Pt 5, 1552–1564.

Parr, D. (1959). Some Manifestations of Hysteria. International Journal of Clinical Practice, 13. https://doi.org/10.1111/j.1742 -1241.1959.tb03752.x.

Perley, M., & Guze, S. (1962). Hysteria--the stability and usefulness of clinical criteria. A quantitative study based on a follow-up period of six to eight years in 39 patients.. The New England journal of medicine, 266, 421-6 . https://doi.org/10.1056/NEJ M196203012660901.

Reed, J. (1975). The diagnosis of 'hysteria'. Psychological Medicine, 5, 13 - 17. https://doi.org/10.1017/S0033291700007170.

Sacks, O. (2012). An anthropologist on Mars: Seven paradoxical tales. Knopf.

CHAPTER SIX

ICONIC CASES AND CULTURAL PORTRAYALS OF HYSTERIA

Iconic Cases: A Voyage into the Historical Narrative of Hysteria

The investigation of renowned legal cases within the historical tapestry of hysteria affords a compelling perspective to scrutinize its comprehension's evolution. As we immerse ourselves in the resonant influence of early psychoanalytic illustrations, most notably the foundational case study of Anna O., one becomes enraptured by the genesis of psychoanalysis and the transformation of psychiatric thought (Lerner, 2010). The intricate narratives surrounding these iconic cases not only illuminate individual odysseys but also serve as a portal to understanding the broader socio-cultural frameworks that shaped the discourse on hysteria. By analyzing these cases, we glean insights into the deeply ingrained beliefs, value systems, and biases that prevailed during various epochs, elucidating their profound impact on the interpretation and categorization of symptoms associated with hysteria (Mason & Przy-było, 2014). Furthermore, the exploration of these pivotal cases highlights the essential role played by trailblazing psychiatrists and psychologists in furthering the understanding of hysteria, aiding its metamorphosis into contemporary mental health diagnoses (Akavia, 2005; Showalter, 1997). A nuanced understanding of these cases is paramount for appreciating the complexities of diagnosing and treating hysteria.

Moreover, the examination of iconic cases enables us to discern the transition of hysteria's conceptualization—from a predominantly corporeal affliction to an emotionally driven condition—thereby underscoring the monumental influence of psychological theories in the domain of mental health (Dmytriw, 2014). These captivating narratives stand as historical benchmarks in the trajectory of hysteria's representation, mirroring the unfolding of progressive attitudes toward mental health and the recognition of patients' lived experiences (Carveth & Carveth, 2004). Through this exhaustive investigation, we can perceive how these extraordinary cases generated ripple effects across medical, psychological, and cultural spheres, affirming the significance and lasting potency of iconic cases in informing our contemporary grasp of hysteria and related mental health disorders.

Case Study: Anna O. and the Genesis of Psychoanalysis

Anna O., the moniker adopted by Bertha Pappenheim, occupies a pivotal position in the annals of psychoanalytic history. Her case laid the groundwork for myriad revolutionary theories within the realm of psychology (Lerner, 2010). Born into affluence in late 19th-century Vienna, Anna O.'s life unfolded amid a backdrop of conflict and trauma. At the age of 21, she manifested an array of enigmatic symptoms that perplexed the medical fraternity (Critchley & Cantor, 1984). Plagued by paralysis, vision disturbances, and myriad somatic ailments, Anna O. became the patient of Dr. Josef Breuer, a distinguished Austrian psychiatrist. What ensued was a historic partnership that would irrevocably alter the landscape of modern psychology. Dr. Breuer's avant-garde methodology, which he dubbed the 'talking cure,' emerged as a precursor to contemporary talk therapy (Showalter, 1997). Through a succession of therapeutic sessions, Anna O. divulged her experiences and traumas, unveiling a discernible pattern of psychological distress entwined with her past. This investigative approach to unearthing repressed memories and emotions paved the way for the advent of psychoanalysis as conceptualized by Dr. Sigmund Freud (Arnold, 2000).

Anna O.'s case not only transformed the comprehension of mental illness but also furnished crucial insights into the unconscious mind and the notion of repression (Crimlisk, 1998). Her symptoms, which eluded conventional medical rationalization, were construed as manifestations of deeply entrenched psychological conflicts (Przybyło & Holly, 2014). These revelations ultimately sculpted the foundational tenets of psychoanalysis, introducing critical concepts such as transference, free association, and the Oedipus complex (Mason & Przybyło, 2014). Additionally, Anna O.'s case accentuated the importance of childhood experiences and their enduring ramifications on an individual's psychological well-being (Lerner, 2010). The profound repercussions of this case study extended far beyond the confines of clinical psychology, infiltrating cultural and societal attitudes toward mental health. The legacy of Anna O. endures within the chronicles of psychology, a testament to the enduring significance of personal narratives in the exploration of the human psyche.

Hysteria in Art: The Illustrated Woman

Hysteria has long entranced artists across many mediums with its convoluted and enigmatic manifestations (Dmytriw, 2014). The archetype of the 'hysterical woman' has repeatedly emerged as a theme within art history, encompassing countless representations that articulate the turmoil and mystery surrounding this condition. Artists have wielded their creative prowess to visually encapsulate hysteria, frequently employing symbolic imagery to portray the inner malaise experienced by affected individuals (Showalter, 1997). Through their artistic creations, they have endeavored to decipher the psychological depths of hysteria, investigating the fragile interplay of strength and vulnerability, chaos and order, within the afflicted psyche.

In the art of the nineteenth century, hysteria was often illustrated through female figures ensnared in various states of distress, their body language and facial expressions conveying acute emotional turmoil (Vine, 2010). Symbolism was pivotal in these representations, with disordered furniture, disheveled attire, and tumultuous surroundings serving as potent emblematic markers of internal chaos and societal disorder (Critchley & Cantor, 1984). The application of color and light further enhanced the symbolic complexity, where vibrant hues encapsulated feelings of passion and despair, while stark contrasts delineated the dichotomy of inner conflict.

As the modern era unfolded, artists persisted in exploring hysteria's complexities, employing diverse styles and techniques to embody the multifaceted nature of this condition (Carveth & Carveth, 2004). Notably, Surrealist artists endeavored to encapsulate the subconscious dimensions of hysteria, utilizing dreamlike imagery and abstract forms to articulate the fragmented psyche of the hysterical individual (Showalter, 1997). These visual renditions frequently blurred the lines between reality and imagination, inviting viewers to contemplate the intricate workings of the human mind when beset by hysteria.

Moreover, the inquiry into hysteria within artistic expressions transcends traditional visual arts, extending to performance art, installations, and multimedia ventures (Mason & Przybyło, 2014). Contemporary artists have embraced interdisciplinary methodologies to navigate the confluence of hysteria with technology, society, and identity, crafting immersive environments that compel audiences to confront the visceral ramifications of emotional upheaval (Dmytriw, 2014). Through interactive showcases and multimedia installations, these creators seek to deepen the awareness of the profound effects of hysteria on both individuals and society collectively. Ultimately, the artistic portrayal of hysteria stands as a testament to the enduring intrigue and relevance of this intricate phenomenon.

Artists consistently proffer poignant reflections on the human condition, illuminating the intricacies of hysteria through evocative imagery and profound symbolism (Showalter, 1997). Their works transcend temporal boundaries, inviting contemplation and introspection while enriching our understanding of hysteria and its persistent presence within our collective consciousness.

Cultural Representation in Literature: Hysterical Heroines

Within the literary realm, the depiction of hysterical heroines emerges as a recurring motif that both reflects and molds societal perceptions of women and mental health. These portrayals frequently depict female protagonists grappling with internal and external discord, subverting conventional ideals of feminine composure and conformity (Mason & Przybyło, 2014). An examination of assorted literary works reveals nuanced representations of hysteria and its ramifications.

The inception of hysterical heroines in literature traces its lineage to classical texts, where seminal female figures such as Antigone and Medea exhibited characteristics that defied the extant gender norms and confronted socio-cultural oppression (Dmytriw, 2014). Transitioning into the modern era, iconic characters such as the protagonist in Charlotte Perkins Gilman's 'The Yellow Wallpaper' poignantly exemplify the struggle against patriarchal constraints, culminating in a descent into mental anguish (Critchley & Cantor, 1984). Such depictions act as incisive commentaries on the power dynamics embedded within society and their consequent impact on women's psychological well-being.

Moreover, the representation of hysterical heroines extends beyond singular narratives, permeating diverse genres, including gothic fiction, feminist literature, and contemporary dystopian narratives. These portrayals not only illuminate the intricacies of female experiences but also reveal the broader cultural and historical contexts that sculpt perceptions of hysteria (Vine, 2010). Additionally, scrutinizing the intersection of literature and mental health facilitates critical engagement with prevailing stereotypes and misconceptions surrounding women's emotional expressions and psychological disorders.

Dissecting the portrayal of hysterical heroines reveals that these literary constructs serve as beacons for discourse on gender, power, and autonomy (Carveth & Carveth, 2004). As readers navigate these characters' narratives and inner landscapes, they are compelled to confront ingrained biases and preconceptions surrounding women's lived realities and emotional tribulations (Dmytriw, 2014). Consequently, the depiction of hysterical heroines emerges as a potent instrument in dismantling stigmatizing attitudes toward mental health and fostering empathy and understanding. Thus, the examination of cultural expressions of hysteria in literature, particularly through the prism of hysterical heroines, affords a multifaceted lens on the intrinsic relationship between gender, literature, and mental health, promoting a more inclusive and compassionate dialogue surrounding these complex issues.

Theatrical Depictions: Drama and Hysteria on Stage

The depiction of hysteria in theatrical productions has long engendered fascination and controversy (Arnold, 2000). From the classic tragedies of ancient Greece to modern theatrical showcases, the representation of hysterical characters has mesmerized audiences and incited discourse on mental health. This segment shall delve into the profound ramifications of dramatic portrayals of hysteria in shaping societal perceptions.

The stage affords a unique arena for probing into the intricacies of hysteria, enabling multidimensional portrayals that transcend the confines of mere textual expression (Crimlisk, 1998). Characters exhibiting hysterical symptoms often occupy the epicenter of profound emotional and psychological disarray, providing rich material for playwrights to explore themes such as gender dynamics, repressed desires, and the straitjackets of societal norms. These portrayals possess the capacity to either challenge or reinforce extant attitudes toward mental health.

The works of illustrious playwrights such as Henrik Ibsen, Tennessee Williams, and Sarah Kane have prominently featured characters entangled with hysteria, offering audiences a thought-provoking lens through which to scrutinize the human condition (Dmytriw, 2014). The staging and performance of hysteria necessitate a delicate equilibrium, as actors must deftly navigate the intricate nuances of the condition while eschewing sensationalism or caricature. The interplay of physicality, vocal modulation, and subtlety in movement all contribute to compelling portrayals that resonate with the audience.

Moreover, the dynamic between the hysterical character and other figures within the narrative illuminates broader social and cultural issues, thus underscoring the significance of these depictions beyond individual psychological struggles (Arnold, 2000). Nevertheless, it is imperative to acknowledge that inaccurate or exaggerated portrayals of hysteria on stage may perpetuate detrimental stereotypes and misconceptions. Hence, ethical considerations regarding the representation of mental health conditions warrant careful navigation by playwrights, directors, and performers.

By critically elucidating the history and impact of theatrical depictions of hysteria, we unearth valuable insights into the evolution of societal attitudes toward mental health and the enduring power of storytelling to shape our comprehension of multifaceted human experiences.

Hysteria in Film: A Cinematic Exploration

In the realm of cinema, hysteria serves as a compelling narrative device intricately woven into myriad genres and storylines (Mason & Przybyło, 2014). From classic black-and-white dramas to contemporary blockbusters, the representation of hysteria on-screen has evolved in tandem with shifting societal attitudes toward mental health. This cinematic exploration frequently delves into the complexities of human emotion, psychological turmoil, and societal perception. Filmmakers harness a diverse array of visual and narrative techniques to depict the manifestations of hysteria, effectively capturing the visceral impact on both characters and audiences.

One predominant theme in cinematic portrayals of hysteria is the intersection of gender dynamics and mental well-being. Numerous films scrutinize how societal expectations and pressures contribute to the emergence of hysteria, particularly among female characters (Vine, 2010). Whether set against historical backdrops or modern landscapes, these narratives illuminate the emotional struggles and societal constraints faced by individuals grappling with hysteria.

Furthermore, cinema adeptly employs its visual lexicon to convey the visceral essence of hysteria. Through evocative cinematography, meticulous sound design, and powerful performances, filmmakers craft haunting and poignant portrayals that immerse viewers in the tumultuous inner lives of characters (Dmytriw, 2014). These representations often capture the dissonance between internal chaos and external composure, offering nuanced insights into the multifaceted experiences of those affected by hysteria.

Notably, the depiction of hysteria in film intersects significantly with broader discussions on power dynamics, agency, and self-advocacy. Characters navigating the throes of hysteria frequently confront profound questions regarding autonomy, authority, and the stigma associated with mental illness (Showalter, 1997). By presenting the intricacies of hysteria within varied sociocultural contexts, filmmakers cultivate critical dialogue around mental health, representation, and the essential pursuit of understanding and empathy.

Moreover, evaluating the evolution of cinematic representations of hysteria facilitates exploring shifting narratives surrounding mental health. As cultural perceptions have evolved, so too have the cinematic portrayals of hysteria, reflecting changing ideologies and sensitivities (Carveth & Carveth, 2004). From early depictions fraught with misconceptions to more nuanced and empathetic renderings, the cinematic landscape presents a tapestry of narratives that mirror society's evolving relationship with mental well-being.

In summation, the cinematic exploration of hysteria is a potent avenue for examining the interplay between individual experiences, societal influences, and artistic interpretation. Through evocative storytelling and empathetic character studies, films enrich the broader discourse on mental health, inviting audiences to engage with the complexities of hysteria and its profound impact on individuals and societies.

The Role of Media: Hysteria in Print and Broadcast

The portrayal of hysteria in print and broadcast media has significantly influenced public perceptions of mental health (Showalter, 1997). Throughout history, the depiction of hysterical behavior in newspapers, magazines, and televised broadcasts has frequently perpetuated stereotypes and misconceptions. Print media, noted for its extensive reach, has historically sensationalized narratives of hysteria, focusing on dramatic and sensational elements to captivate readers (Crimlisk, 1998). The use of hyperbolic language and striking imagery contributes to a dehumanizing portrayal of individuals experiencing hysteria, reinforcing stigmatizing attitudes in society.

Similarly, broadcast media, including television and radio, has been crucial in perpetuating sensationalized narratives surrounding hysteria. Television programs and news segments often prioritize shocking or exaggerated depictions of mental health issues, which may contribute to a lack of understanding and compassion (Dmytriw, 2014). Furthermore, broadcast portrayals of hysteria frequently overlook the intricate psychological foundations of the condition, opting instead for simplistic and often inaccurate representations.

However, as societal awareness of mental health continues to progress, there is a burgeoning effort to challenge these damaging portrayals within both print and broadcast media (Mason & Przybyło, 2014). Advocacy groups and mental health organizations strive to raise awareness about the ramifications of stigmatizing narratives while promoting more responsible storytelling. Additionally, initiatives aimed at fostering accurate and sensitive depictions of mental health conditions have gained traction, resulting in the inclusion of diverse and authentic portrayals of individuals with hysteria in both print and broadcast formats.

This shift toward enhanced authenticity and sensitivity in media representations signifies an essential stride in combating stigma and nurturing a more compassionate understanding of mental health. By acknowledging the pervasive influence of media portrayals and proactively advocating for accurate and empathetic storytelling, society can cultivate a culture that respects and supports individuals affected by hysteria and other mental health conditions.

Comparison of Global Interpretations: West Meets East

Examining the global interpretations of hysteria necessitates appreciating the stark contrasts in how Western and Eastern cultures have historically perceived and represented this multifaceted phenomenon (Lerner, 2010). Western interpretations of hysteria have often been shaped by Freudian psychoanalysis and the medicalization of mental illness, while Eastern perspectives may draw from traditional medicine and cultural philosophies. Understanding these divergent viewpoints significantly enhances our comprehension of hysteria and its broader societal implications.

In Western societies, hysteria has predominantly been approached through a psychological and psychiatric lens, intertwining with evolving frameworks of mental health diagnosis and treatment (Akavia, 2005). The pioneering influences of figures such as Freud and Charcot have solidified the portrayal of hysteria as a primarily feminine affliction within Western contexts (Dmytriw, 2014). In contrast, Eastern conceptualizations of mental distress often encompass holistic approaches, integrating traditional healing practices and sophisticated understandings of mind-body connections (Dmytriw, 2014).

Exploring historical texts—such as ancient Asian medical treatises and philosophical writings—affords an opportunity to examine how hysteria has been conceived and addressed within diverse Eastern traditions (Gullhaugen & Nøttestad, 2011). From the perspectives of traditional Chinese medicine or Ayurveda, hysteria may be viewed through the lens of energy imbalances or disruptions in the body's vital forces, offering a striking contrast to the Western focus on neurosis and subconscious turmoil (Mason & Przybyło, 2014).

Moreover, delving into cultural artifacts like folklore, mythology, and indigenous healing practices reveals the symbolic representations of hysteria in Eastern contexts. These narratives frequently intersect with broader themes of spirituality, ancestry, and communal well-being, presenting a markedly different narrative than the individualized, clinically oriented discourse prevalent in the West (Showalter, 1997).

The dynamic interplay between these differing interpretations underscores the richness and complexity of understanding hysteria on a global scale. It accentuates the intersection of culture, history, and belief systems in shaping mental health narratives (Crimlisk, 1998). By critically scrutinizing these disparities, we gain insights into the potential limitations of our contemporary understanding of hysteria and the pressing need for a more inclusive, culturally sensitive approach to mental health discourse.

Critique and Analysis: Misrepresentation and Stereotypes

The portrayal of hysteria across various cultural contexts has oftentimes led to misrepresentation and the reinforcement of stereotypes, affecting global perceptions of mental health (Carveth &

Carveth, 2004). A comparison of Western interpretations with those from Eastern cultures reveals that countless depictions have perpetuated misconceptions surrounding hysteria. Western portrayals, particularly in literature and media, frequently conflate hysteria with femininity, bolstering the stereotype of women as emotionally unstable or irrational (Przybyło & Holly, 2014). Conversely, Eastern interpretations may associate hysteria with spiritual or supernatural dimensions, contributing to an alternative set of stereotypes (Arnold, 2000).

Despite these differences, both representations tend to overlook the complexities and nuances inherent in this mental health condition. The inclination to sensationalize and simplify hysteria for dramatic effect leads to perpetuating harmful stereotypes (Crimlisk, 1998). Furthermore, these portrayals often neglect the individual experiences and struggles of those afflicted by hysteria, reducing them to mere caricatures or narrative devices (Dmytriw, 2014). This oversimplification can critically affect how individuals displaying similar symptoms are perceived and treated, exacerbating stigmatization and misunderstanding.

Additionally, the prevalence of inaccurate representations in popular culture contributes to the persistence of stereotypes that impede progress in destigmatizing mental health issues (Mason & Przybyło, 2014). It is imperative to rigorously examine and challenge these misrepresentations and stereotypes while emphasizing the necessity for nuanced and empathetic portrayals of individuals navigating conditions such as hysteria. By illuminating the limitations of past depictions, we can foster a more informed and inclusive understanding of mental health in society (Vine, 2010). Through deliberate efforts to present diverse and authentic narratives, we can mitigate the detrimental effects of misrepresentation and stereotypes, paving the way toward greater compassion and support for individuals grappling with mental health challenges (Lerner, 2010).

Conclusion: Impacts on Current Perceptions of Mental Health

The portrayal of hysteria in iconic cases and cultural representations has profoundly influenced contemporary perceptions of mental health, particularly concerning women. These historical depictions have contributed to the stigmatization of mental illness, perpetuating misconceptions and stereotypes that continue to affect individuals seeking help today (Mason & Przybyło, 2014). By analyzing the historical context of hysteria and its representation across various mediums, we can glean insights into the enduring impacts on current mental health perceptions.

A significant impact of these cultural portrayals is the reinforcement of gendered attitudes toward mental illness. The association of hysteria with women, especially during the 19th and early 20th centuries, has resulted in persistent biases surrounding the understanding and treatment of mental health disorders (Showalter, 1997). This bias has generated disparities in diagnosis, treatment, and social acceptance, creating barriers for individuals—especially women—navigating the intricate landscape of mental health care.

Moreover, the propagation of stereotypes and misrepresentations through cultural mediums has obstructed the destigmatization of mental illness (Dmytriw, 2014). Sensationalized and often inaccurate portrayals of hysteria in literature, art, theater, and film contribute to a lack of understanding and empathy toward individuals experiencing mental health challenges (Arnold, 2000). This trend reinforces societal tendencies to dismiss or trivialize the struggles of those with mental health disorders, hampering efforts to cultivate a more inclusive and supportive atmosphere for those in need.

In light of these observations, it is vital to recognize the long-lasting repercussions of historical narratives surrounding hysteria and their impact on modern perceptions of mental health.

By acknowledging the detrimental consequences of misrepresentation and stereotypes, we can strive to reshape public attitudes and champion a more compassionate, informed approach to mental illness (Przybyło & Holly, 2014). This endeavor involves fostering awareness of the deep-rooted influences of past cultural representations and confronting ingrained biases to engender a more equitable and empathetic society (Crimlisk, 1998).

Collaboration among individuals, healthcare professionals, and advocates is essential to dismantle the enduring effects of historical inaccuracies and stigma. Initiatives aimed at redefining mental health narratives, highlighting diverse experiences, and amplifying marginalized voices are critical to reshaping public perceptions (Vine, 2010). Through education, advocacy, and representation, we can cultivate a culture of understanding, support, and acceptance for those encountering mental health challenges, transcending the limitations imposed by historical misrepresentations and stereotypes. Ultimately, actively addressing the influences of iconic cases and cultural portrayals of hysteria on contemporary perceptions of mental health is crucial in promoting holistic well-being and fostering a society that embraces the complexities of the human experience.

In a Nutshell:

Hysteria, historically considered a predominantly female disorder, has been a subject of medical, psychological, and cultural discourse for centuries. Originating from the works of Charcot and Freud, hysteria has evolved in its representation and understanding, manifesting in various forms across different cultural contexts. This synthesis explores iconic cases and cultural portrayals of hysteria, drawing insights from multiple research papers.

Key Insights

- **Cultural Resurgence and Media Portrayals**:

  - Hysteria has seen a resurgence in cultural representations, appearing in films, plays, and media coverage, reflecting ongoing societal anxieties and cultural norms.

  - Modern portrayals often detach hysteria from its historical gender and medical connotations, instead framing it as a broader social and psychological phenomenon.

- **Historical and Modern Forms**:

  - Charcot's original descriptions of hysteria, including conditions like la grande hystérie and hysterical hemianaesthesia, remain relevant, with similar cases still observed in certain communities.

  - Contemporary forms of hysteria include conditions like chronic fatigue syndrome, multiple personality disorder, and Gulf War syndrome, which are seen as modern manifestations of the disorder.

- **Psychoanalytic and Feminist Perspectives**:

  - Freud's case studies, such as the Dora case, highlight the intersection of hysteria with gender conflicts and societal norms, with some feminist interpretations viewing hysteria as a form of resistance against patriarchal oppression.

- ○ Hysteria is often seen as a communicative interaction within familial and social systems, reflecting deeper psychological and social dynamics.

- **Cultural and Intellectual Constructs**:

  - ○ Hysteria is described as a complex interplay between mind and body, health and illness, and cultural representations, often defying simple categorization.

  - ○ The disorder is framed as a language of death and a cultural construct that requires a holistic understanding of its historical, medical, and performative aspects.

- **Historical Continuity and Evolution**:

  - ○ Despite changes in medical diagnoses and social conditions, hysteria has persisted in various forms, reflecting its deep-rooted presence in cultural and psychological narratives.

  - ○ The disorder's history is marked by its mysterious appearances and disappearances, influenced by evolving social and medical contexts.

Conclusion

Hysteria, both as a medical condition and a cultural phenomenon, has undergone significant transformations over the centuries. Its portrayal in media and literature continues to reflect societal anxieties and cultural norms. While historical cases by Charcot and Freud laid the groundwork, modern interpretations, and manifestations highlight the disorder's enduring relevance. Understanding hysteria requires a multidisciplinary approach, considering its complex interplay of psychological, social, and cultural factors.

References

Akavia, N. (2005). Hysteria, Identification, and the Family: A Rereading of Freud's Dora Case. American Imago, 62, 193 - 216. https://doi.org/10.1353/AIM.2005.0021.

Arnold, D. (2000). The knotted subject: hysteria and its discontents. Medical History, 44, 290 - 291. https://doi.org/10.1017/S002572730006662X.

Carveth, D., & Carveth, J. (2004). Fugitives from Guilt: Postmodern De-Moralization and the New Hysterias. American Imago, 60, 445 - 479. https://doi.org/10.1353/AIM.2004.0002.

Crimlisk, H. (1998). Hystories: Hysterical Epidemics and Modern Culture By Elaine Showalter. London: Picador. 1997. 244 pp. £19.99 (hb). ISBN 0-3303467-09. British Journal of Psychiatry, 173, 90 - 90. https://doi.org/10.1192/S0007125000150718.

Critchley, E., & Cantor, H. (1984). Charcot's hysteria renaissance. British Medical Journal (Clinical research ed.), 289, 1785 - 1788. https://doi.org/10.1136/BMJ.289.6460.1785.

Dmytriw, A. (2014). Gender and Sex Manifestations in Hysteria Across Medicine and the Arts. European Neurology, 73, 44–50.

Gullhaugen, A. S., & Nøttestad, J. A. (2011). Looking for the Hannibal Behind the Cannibal: Current Status of Case Research. International Journal of Offender Therapy and Comparative Criminology, 55, 350–369.

Lerner, P. (2010). Andrew Scull, Hysteria: the biography, Biographies of Disease Series, Oxford University Press, 2009, pp. 223, £12.99, $24.95 (hardback 978-0-19-956096-7). Medical History, 54, 546 - 547. https://doi.org/10.1017/S0025727300006487.

Mason, D., & Przybyło, E. (2014). Hysteria Manifest: Cultural Lives of a Great Disorder. ESC: English Studies in Canada, 40, 1 - 18. https://doi.org/10.1353/ESC.2014.0003.

Przybyło, E., & Holly, M. (2014). Seeing Hysteria: A Case, A Study. ESC: English Studies in Canada, 40, 177 - 188. https://doi.org/10.1353/ESC.2014.0007.

Showalter, E. (1997). Hystories: Hysterical epidemics and modern media. Columbia University Press.

Showalter, E. (1997). Hystories: Hysterical Epidemics and Modern Culture. . https://doi.org/10.5860/choice.35-0946.

Vine, S. (2010). 'Sublime Anamnesis: Hysteria and Temporality in Thomas's "The White Hotel."' Nineteenth-Century Literature, 56, 196-220. https://doi.org/10.1215/0041462X-2010-3006.

CHAPTER SEVEN

EVOLUTION OF HYSTERIA: TRANSITION TO CONTEMPORARY DIAGNOSES

The Historical Complexities of Hysteria and Its Implications for Women's Health

Historically, the notion of hysteria is ensconced in societal perceptions that scrutinize women and their corporeal realities. The etymology of "hysteria" traces back to the ancient Greek term "hysteria," meaning uterus, illuminating the age-old belief that this affliction was confined to women and intertwined with their reproductive systems (Micale, 2008). Over the centuries, women exhibiting a diverse array of symptoms—ranging from anxiety and melancholia to syncope and ambiguous somatic complaints—were frequently categorized as hysterical.

The comprehension of hysteria has transformed markedly across epochs, molded by the dominant cultural and medical doctrines of various times. Notably, the 19th century witnessed pivotal advancements in the medical interpretation of hysteria, profoundly influenced by the pioneering research of prominent figures, including Jean-Martin Charcot and Sigmund Freud. Through his investigations at the Salpêtrière Hospital in Paris, Charcot concentrated on the tangible manifestations of hysteria, significantly shaping the nascent neurological perspective of this condition (Cramer, 2018).

Conversely, Sigmund Freud, the eminent psychoanalyst, ventured into the intricate psychological dimensions of hysteria. His theories delved into the unconscious conflicts and traumas believed to underlie the condition, positing that this emotional turmoil and psychological strife were pivotal in its articulation (Chodoff, 1974). Freud's clinical work with individuals manifesting hysterical symptoms culminated in the genesis of psychoanalysis as a therapeutic modality, illuminating the intricate interplay of psychological, emotional, and physical dimensions of mental distress (Bruno et al., 2020).

However, hysteria exemplifies a broader societal trend of the medicalization and pathologization of women's experiences. Women who diverged from traditional behavioral norms—whether by voicing robust emotions, contesting male authority, or exhibiting nonconformist behaviors—were often hastily diagnosed with hysteria (Tasca et al., 2012). This stigmatization reinforced rigid gender roles and upheld a patriarchal social framework, relegating women's genuine expressions of autonomy and individuality to the realm of mental pathology (Lader & Sartorius, 1968).

As medical scholarship progressed and diagnostic standards became more consistent, the label of "hysteria" gradually waned in the field of mental health. The once-common symptoms associated with hysteria have since been reallocated to varying diagnostic classifications. The Diagnostic and Statistical Manual of Mental Disorders (DSM) no longer recognizes hysteria as a distinct diagnosis, opting instead to categorize conditions that encapsulate symptoms historically attributed to it (Webster, 2023).

One such contemporary classification is somatic symptom disorder, characterized by an intense focus on physical symptoms that may lack a clear medical basis (Malcomson, 1968). This diagnosis acknowledges the tangible suffering experienced by individuals while integrating psychological influences that might exacerbate their symptoms. Furthermore, the understanding of dissociative disorders has advanced to incorporate symptoms once deemed hysterical, including dissociative amnesia and dissociative identity disorder (Stefanis et al., 1976).

The metamorphosis from hysteria to modern diagnostic criteria exemplifies a significant shift within mental health toward evidence-based, person-centered paradigms. Recognizing that individuals of all genders can experience phenomena traditionally attributed to hysteria has engendered a more nuanced and equitable approach to diagnostic practices. This evolution has been instrumental in diminishing stigma and ensuring equitable access to effective mental health treatment for diverse populations (Lucas, 2009).

Moreover, it is imperative to acknowledge sociocultural dynamics' historical and persisting influences on mental health. The pathologization of women's experiences, as illustrated by hysteria, serves as a poignant reminder of the intricate ways in which gender, power relations, and societal expectations mold the perceptions and management of mental suffering. This awareness accentuates the necessity for a comprehensive and inclusive framework in mental health care that addresses the intersecting ramifications of gender, culture, and identity (Villalpando et al., 2005).

By scrutinizing the evolution of hysteria, we unearth the complexities surrounding mental health diagnostics and treatment alongside the broader societal forces that inform our interpretation of mental distress (Cramer, 2018). This understanding reinforces the call for a holistic paradigm in mental health that embraces individuals' diverse experiences and requirements, transcending barriers of gender, ethnicity, or social context.

The convoluted history of hysteria also underscores the critical need to examine the intersections of power, privilege, and marginalized identities within the mental health discourse. The historical pathologization of women's experiences elucidates how societal norms and power dynamics can skew perceptions of mental distress, perpetuating deleterious stereotypes and inhibiting access to appropriate care (Tasca et al., 2012). This acknowledgment further emphasizes the urgency of advocating for mental health practices that are attentive to all individuals' varied experiences and needs.

Moreover, the concept of hysteria invites a broader contemplation of the ramifications associated with the medicalization and pathologization of certain experiences, particularly those tied to gender and identity (Bruno et al., 2020). It prompts a reevaluation of how societal expectations and power frameworks shape both the diagnosis and treatment of mental health conditions, as well as the lived realities of individuals confronting mental turmoil. Recognizing these complexities mandates a fundamental reassessment of mental health methodologies to ensure inclusivity, equity, and responsiveness to the diverse spectrum of individual needs.

In summation, the historical trajectory of hysteria offers invaluable insights into the intricate interplay of health, culture, and power dynamics (Micale, 2008). By critically examining the origins and evolution of hysteria, we can enrich our understanding of mental health while striving towards more compassionate, culturally attuned modalities of care. This journey of inquiry and introspection aspires to cultivate a more inclusive, equitable, and empathetic landscape for mental health support and intervention, fostering a society that values the diversity of human experience in its entirety.

In a Nutshell:

Evolution of Hysteria: Transition to Contemporary Diagnoses

The concept of hysteria has undergone significant transformations from its early descriptions to contemporary psychiatric diagnoses. Historically, hysteria was often linked to women and attributed to various causes, including repressed sexuality and psychological trauma. Over time, the understanding and classification of hysteria have evolved, leading to its redefinition and the emergence of new diagnostic categories.

Key Insights from Research Papers

- **Historical Perspectives and Early Theories**:

    - Hysteria was initially described by Briquet in 1859 and later conceptualized as a conversion symptom and a hysterical personality.

    - Early theories linked hysteria to the wandering womb, demon possession, and repressed sexual emotions.

- **Psychoanalytic Contributions**:

    - Freud and Breuer's work on hysteria emphasized the role of repressed traumatic memories and the cleavage of consciousness.

- Lacan viewed hysteria as a neurosis that reflects the struggle between individual neurosis and civilization, using the case of Dora to refine his theories.

- **Decline and Reclassification in Modern Psychiatry**:

  - The diagnosis of hysteria has seen a decline, with a significant decrease in patients diagnosed with hysteria and an increase in mixed conversion symptoms.

  - The term "hysteria" was removed from the DSM-III in 1980, reflecting a shift towards more specific diagnoses like conversion disorder and somatoform disorders.

- **Contemporary Diagnoses and New Clinical Entities**:

  - Hysteria has evolved into diagnoses such as psychogenic non-epileptic seizures (PNES), which are paroxysmal manifestations related to unconscious psychogenic processes.

  - Modern psychiatry often reclassifies symptoms previously attributed to hysteria under dissociative and somatoform disorders.

- **Criticism and Clinical Challenges**:

  - The diagnosis of hysteria has been criticized for leading to clinical errors and complacency, with many cases later found to have organic or well-defined psychiatric disorders.

○ The concept of conversion of psychic energy has been challenged for lacking biological foundation and experimental evidence.

Conclusion

The evolution of hysteria from its early descriptions to contemporary psychiatric diagnoses reflects significant changes in understanding and classification. Initially linked to repressed sexuality and psychological trauma, hysteria has been redefined and reclassified into more specific diagnostic categories such as conversion disorder and psychogenic non-epileptic seizures. Despite its historical significance, the term "hysteria" has largely been abandoned in modern psychiatry, highlighting the ongoing refinement of psychiatric diagnoses.

References

Briggs, L. (2000). The Race of Hysteria: "Overcivilization" and the "Savage" Woman in Late Nineteenth-Century Obstetrics and Gynecology. American Quarterly, 52, 246 - 273. https://doi.org/10.1353/AQ.2000.0013.

Bruno, J., Machado, J., & Auxéméry, Y. (2020). From epileptic hysteria to psychogenic non-epileptic seizure: Continuity or discontinuity for contemporary psychiatry? European Journal of Trauma & Dissociation, 100190. https://doi.org/10.1016/ j.ejtd.2020.100190.

Chodoff, P. (1974). The diagnosis of hysteria: an overview. The American journal of psychiatry, 131 10, 1073-8. https:// doi.org/10.1176/AJP.131.10.1073.

Cramer, P. (2018). What Has Happened to Hysteria? Journal of Nervous & Mental Disease. https://doi.org/10.1097/N MD.0000000000000850.

Lader, M., & Sartorius, N. (1968). Anxiety in patients with hysterical conversion symptoms. Journal of Neurology, Neurosurgery & Psychiatry, 31, 490 - 495. https://doi.org/10.113 6/jnnp.31.5.490.

Lucas, V. (2009). Studies on Hysteria. BMJ: British Medical Journal, 338. https://doi.org/10.1136/BMJ.B989.

Malcomson, K. (1968). Globus Hystericus Vel Pharyngis. The Journal of Laryngology & Otology, 82, 219 - 230. http s://doi.org/10.1017/S0022215100068687.

Micale, M. S. (2008). Hysteria: The history of a disease. Princeton University Press.

Stefanis, C., Markidis, M., & Christodoulou, G. (1976). Observations on the Evolution of the Hysterical Symptomatology.

British Journal of Psychiatry, 128, 269 - 275. https://doi.org/10.
1192/bjp.128.3.269.

Tasca, C., Rapetti, M., Carta, M., & Fadda, B. (2012). Women
And Hysteria In The History Of Mental Health. Clinical Practice
and Epidemiology in Mental Health: CP & EMH, 8, 110 - 119.
https://doi.org/10.2174/1745017901208010110.

Villalpando, M. I. B., Sotres, J. C., Manning, H. G., & González,
A. S. (2005). La fibromialgia: ¿un Síndrome Somático Funcional
o una nueva conceptualización de la histeria? Análisis cuali-cuan-
titativo. Salud Mental, 28, 41–50.

Webster, J. (2023). The Most Hysterical Psychoanalyst. Journal
of the American Psychoanalytic Association, 71, 907 - 931. http
s://doi.org/10.1177/00030651231209737.

CHAPTER EIGHT

MEDICALIZATION OF HYSTERIA: PATHOLOGIZING WOMEN'S EMOTIONS

Historical Context: The Medical Gaze Toward Women's Health

THE HISTORICAL TRAJECTORY OF women's health has been markedly shaped by the medical gaze, which has evolved in concordance with broader societal paradigms and beliefs. From antiquity to contemporary society, the perception of women's corporeality has been refracted through diverse interpretive frameworks, where prevailing cultural norms have frequently influenced medical ideologies. In ancient civilizations—such as those of Egypt, Mesopotamia, Greece, and Rome—the comprehension of women's health was inextricably linked to mythological and superstitious thought and religious dogmas. For instance, the ancient Greek notion of the 'wandering womb' exemplifies early medical endeavors to elucidate female physiology within the confines of predominantly patriarchal constructs (Risse, 1988). As societal paradigms transitioned into the medieval and Renaissance epochs, the incursion of Christian doctrine and the burgeoning of academic institutions began to increasingly mold medical discourse. Women's health became entangled in moral and spiritual frameworks, ultimately leading to the pathologization of natural biological processes, including menstruation and childbirth. Moreover, the emergence of hysteria—derived from the Greek term for uterus—during this period laid the groundwork for centuries of medical scrutiny regarding women's emotional and behavioral expressions (Layne, 2019).

The 19th century heralded significant advancements in psychiatry and neurology, with luminaries such as Jean-Martin Charcot and Sigmund Freud propelling the medicalization of female psychological experiences. This era witnessed the institutionalization of hysteria as a psychiatric diagnosis, reinforcing the premise that women's emotional expressions were symptomatic of latent mental disorders (Hooper, 2019). Notably, the medical perspective on women's health evolved concurrently with substantial socio-political shifts, including the suffrage movement and transformations in gender dynamics. As women began to contest traditional norms and advocate for greater autonomy, medical narratives evolved in tandem with these power reconfigurations. Yet, the medicalization of women's emotions endured, often masquerading as scientific objectivity and clinical rigor. A thorough exploration of this historical context reveals the enduring repercussions of societal norms on medical interpretations of women's health, thereby illuminating the intricate interplay between culture, gender, and healthcare (Weitz, 2004).

Defining Medicalization: A Paradigm Shift in Understanding Hysteria

The notion of medicalization signifies an essential inflection point in the historical understanding of hysteria. It denotes the metamorphosis of what was once predominantly perceived as a social or psychological phenomenon into a medical issue (Alves, 2020). Such a paradigm shift carries substantial ramifications for our comprehension of hysteria and, by extension, for the experiences of the women historically labeled with this intricate condition. Central to the medicalization process is the assertion of medical hegemony over phenomena traditionally situated within domains such as morality, religion, or culture. In the context of hysteria, the transition towards medicalization involved the elevation of physicians and healthcare professionals as the principal interpreters and adjudicators of women's emotional and psychological experiences (Tasca et al., 2012). This shift from a multifaceted social conception to a medical one has immense consequences, shaping diagnostic criteria, treatment methodologies, and societal attitudes regarding female emotional expression.

However, the medicalization of hysteria also engenders thought-provoking inquiries into power dynamics and gender biases within the healthcare milieu. It invites a critical evaluation of whose voices and perspectives dominate the construction of diagnostic frameworks and therapeutic interventions (Ussher, 2013). Furthermore, the medicalization of hysteria underscores how broader sociocultural narratives influence the perception and management of women's health issues, thereby highlighting the intricate interconnections of medicine, authority, and gender in the historical discourse surrounding hysteria (Lader & Sartorius, 1968). Additionally, the process of medicalization introduces a dichotomy between normative and pathological emotional states, frequently leading to reductive categorizations of complex human

experiences. Such oversimplification may effectively marginalize authentic emotional distress endured by individuals—especially women—whose manifestations do not conform to established diagnostic criteria (Althaus, 1866). Investigating the
limits of medicalization within the hysteria context challenges
us to consider the inadequacies of medical frameworks in encapsulating the richness and variability of women's emotional
realities, prompting an exploration of alternative, more inclusive models for comprehending and addressing emotional
well-being.

Ultimately, a nuanced understanding of medicalization
within the purview of hysteria necessitates a comprehensive
inquiry into the confluence of medical, social, and cultural
forces that have continually influenced and transformed the
interpretation of women's emotional health. Recognizing the
ramifications of medicalization is indispensable in cultivating a
holistic and empathetic approach to addressing women's psychological well-being—one that acknowledges the intricate nature and individuality of emotional experiences while remain-
ing cognizant of the broader structural and systemic influences
that permeate the medical landscape (Riddell, 2012).

The Role of Physicians and the Medical Community

Historically, physicians and the medical community have
played an instrumental role in shaping perceptions and treatment modalities for hysteria. From the ancient Greeks to the
present times, medical professionals have been pivotal in defining and addressing this enigmatic condition (Watkins, 2000).
The medical paradigm pertaining to hysteria has often been
swayed by societal norms, contemporary ideologies, and evolving perceptions of women's health.

Physicians have traditionally been central figures in codifying the expressive symptoms and manifestations of hysteria, thus contributing to the establishment of diagnostic criteria that have, at times, served to reinforce rather than challenge entrenched gender biases within the mental health domain (Hooper, 2019). The ramifications of the medical community extend beyond mere diagnosis; they envelop the prescription of treatments ranging from therapeutic modalities to pharmacological remedies. The inherent power dynamics in the patient-physician nexus have undeniably influenced how hysteria is framed and addressed in clinical settings.

Moreover, the medicalization of hysteria has facilitated the emergence of specialized fields such as gynecology and psychiatry, which have profoundly shaped the understanding of female psychology and wellness (Pathiraja et al., 2022). These developments have engendered a complex interplay between physiological and psychological paradigms of mental health, often resulting in far-reaching implications for women's experiences within healthcare systems.

The medical community's involvement in legitimizing and pathologizing women's emotional expressions remains significant (Layne, 2019). By positioning themselves as authoritative figures in matters concerning mental and emotional health, physicians have exerted considerable influence over public perceptions and societal attitudes toward women who exhibit symptoms of hysteria. A critical evaluation of the historical context reveals how, at times, medical professionals have unwittingly perpetuated harmful stereotypes and discriminatory practices, thus exacerbating the stigmatization of female emotional expression (Riddell, 2012). Conscientiously scrutinizing the role of physicians and the medical community in the medicalization of hysteria necessitates a nuanced appreciation of how the profession has historically engaged with and contributed to prevailing societal narratives regarding women's mental health. As we advance, it becomes imperative to reassess these dynamics and explore how the medical field can emerge as a positive catalyst in dismantling antiquated perceptions of hysteria, ultimately supporting individuals—regardless of gender—in their journeys toward mental wellness.

Diagnostic Criteria: Establishing Control Over Female Psychology

In the realm of hysteria's medicalization, diagnostic criteria have played a crucial role in perpetuating the subjugation of female psychology. Both in antiquity and contemporary practice, these standards have been wielded as instruments of control over women's emotional and psychological experiences (Tasca et al., 2012). This section endeavors to investigate the historical evolution of diagnostic criteria for hysteria, illuminating the ways in which they have influenced societal perceptions of women's mental health.

The formulation of diagnostic criteria for hysteria has historically been intertwined with prevailing societal attitudes toward women (Ussher, 2013). Such standards often embodied misogynistic ideologies and gendered biases, leading to the pathologization of natural emotional responses characteristic of women. The canonization of symptoms such as anxiety, emotional expression, and assertiveness as markers of hysteria propagated control over female behavior and emotional responses (Lader & Sartorius, 1968).

Furthermore, the development of diagnostic benchmarks for hysteria served to fortify the authority of medical professionals over women's bodies and minds. By delineating specific symptomatology and behavioral patterns as indicative of hysteria, medical practitioners appropriated the power to classify and categorize women based on their conformity or deviation from societal norms (Hooper, 2019). Consequently, this reinforced the perception of women as innately irrational and volatile, thereby justifying the necessity of medical interventions and oversight (Risse, 1988).

Throughout history, the discourse surrounding women's mental health has been fundamentally sculpted by diagnostic criteria for hysteria. The alignment of emotional distress with pathological conditions undermined the authenticity of women's experiences, relegating their feelings to a framework of disorder rather than recognizing them as legitimate responses to social and psychological stressors. As a result, women have frequently found themselves subject to stigmatization and marginalization, further entrenching a cycle of disenfranchisement and vulnerability.

Engaging in a critical examination of the construction and application of diagnostic criteria for hysteria is essential in understanding the pernicious influence of medicalization on women's psychological well-being. Uncovering the historical context and societal foundations of these standards makes it feasible to challenge entrenched systems of control and redefine the frameworks through which women's emotional experiences are interpreted and validated (Weitz, 2004).

Pharmaceutical Interventions and Treatment Practices

The medicalization of hysteria has ushered in a spectrum of pharmaceutical interventions and treatment modalities ostensibly designed to mitigate the symptoms associated with the condition. Pharmacotherapy emerged as a cornerstone of the medical approach to managing hysteria, particularly with the ascendance of psychiatry as a specialized domain (Lader & Sartorius, 1968). Various psychotropic substances were administrated to women diagnosed with this malady, frequently without careful consideration of the underlying etiologies.

One of the more infamous instances involved the employment of opiates and sedatives to regulate the emotional and behavioral manifestations attributed to hysteria. While these medications might have provided a temporary respite from distressing symptoms, they often precipitated dependency and addiction among patients (Watkins, 2000). Similarly, the utilization of tranquilizers and barbiturates aimed to assuage perceived disturbances within female psychology, yet frequently resulted in deleterious side effects and long-term health ramifications.

Moreover, the emergence of psychotropic agents further recalibrated the landscape of pharmacological interventions for hysteria. Antipsychotics and mood stabilizers increasingly found their way into treatment regimens designed to address emotional instability and cognitive irregularities attributed to the condition (Riddell, 2012). However, the indiscriminate administration of these potent substances frequently neglected the unique experiences and contexts of individual patients, raising significant ethical concerns regarding the medicalization process.

In addition to pharmacological remedies, treatment approaches also encompassed various somatic interventions. Surgical procedures like hysterectomies and ovariectomies were advocated, premised on the belief that excising reproductive organs would alleviate the alleged psychological distress experienced by women diagnosed with hysteria (Pathiraja et al., 2022). The widespread acceptance of such invasive procedures underscores the extent to which the medical establishment sought to exert control over female bodies in an effort to manage perceived 'hysterical' behaviors.

A critical appraisal of the historical and contemporary implications of pharmaceutical interventions and treatment practices is paramount to understanding the broader impact of hysteria's medicalization. While certain medications have undoubtedly afforded relief to individuals grappling with genuine psychological distress, the overarching tendency to pathologize and medicate women's emotional experiences raises profound inquiries into gender biases, power dynamics within healthcare, and the ethics of psychiatric interventions. This discourse invites a rigorous examination of the intricate dynamics between pharmaceutical treatments, societal attitudes toward women's mental health, and the enduring legacy of hysteria within medical narratives (Hooper, 2019).

Case Studies: Illustrative Examples of Medical Misunderstandings

Case studies serve as vital illustrations of the intricacies and challenges inherent in the medicalization of hysteria. By examining specific instances, we can gain profound insights into the potential missteps and detrimental consequences that medical interventions can have on women's mental health (Layne, 2019). These narratives elucidate how medical professionals have, at times, misconstrued and pathologized women's emotional experiences, resulting in misdiagnoses, inappropriate treatments, and, ultimately, prolonged suffering.

Consider the case of a young woman who sought assistance for debilitating anxiety and physical symptoms correlated with her menstrual cycle. Despite clear indicators of premenstrual dysphoric disorder (PMDD), her physician dismissed her condition as merely 'normal' hormonal fluctuations (Riddell, 2012). This oversight led to a significant delay in acquiring proper care and an exacerbation of her distressing symptoms, illustrating the perils of underestimating genuine psychiatric issues in favor of reductive and gendered perceptions embedded in medical practice.

Another poignant case involves a middle-aged woman who presented symptoms aligning with generalized anxiety disorder and panic attacks. However, due to entrenched stereotypes regarding female emotional volatility, her distress was hastily categorized as hysteria. This resulted in a stigmatizing diagnosis that overshadowed the true nature of her mental health challenges, emphasizing the dangers inherent in overlooking authentic psychiatric conditions (Tasca et al., 2012).

These examples illuminate the urgent necessity for healthcare providers to undertake comprehensive training aimed at recognizing and addressing mental health concerns without succumbing to historical biases associated with hysteria. They also serve as potent reminders of the profound impact of gender biases within the medical field and highlight the need for a more empathetic, nuanced approach when it comes to understanding and treating women's psychological wellness. Upon further examination of these narratives, we can uncover the multifaceted repercussions of medical misunderstandings and illuminate pathways toward improved understanding and support for individuals coping with mental health challenges.

Critiques of the Medicalization Approach: Voices of Dissent

The medicalization of hysteria, particularly in relation to women's emotional experiences, has attracted substantial scrutiny from a variety of critics. Dissenting voices have emerged on multiple fronts, challenging the fundamental paradigm that pathologizes emotional distress and psychological states primarily encountered by women. A central critique focuses on the gendered implications of medicalization, underscoring its disproportionate impact on women while frequently neglecting the social, cultural, and environmental factors that shape mental well-being (Alves, 2020).

Critics assert that medicalization simplistically reduces complex emotional experiences to rigid diagnostic categories and pharmaceutical treatments (Ussher, 2013). This reductionist approach fails to account for the intricate interplay of sociocultural contexts and individual psychological factors in shaping emotional responses. Additionally, the power dynamics at play in the medicalization process have been a significant focal point of criticism, with many contending that the authority of physicians and mental

health professionals in defining and managing hysteria perpetuates entrenched gender biases and reinforces societal stereotypes
depicting women as excessively emotional or irrational (Hooper,
2019).

Furthermore, concerns arise regarding the ethical ramifications
of categorizing natural emotional responses as pathological. This
labeling can lead to an overreliance on medication while neglecting
alternative, more holistic avenues of support and care for individuals experiencing distress (Weitz, 2004). Another dimension of
dissent includes the stigmatizing effects of medicalization itself;
critics argue that labeling emotional experiences as indicative of a
disorder can marginalize and disempower individuals—especially
women—who seek understanding and validation for their struggles. This critique calls for a more inclusive and empathetic framework, one that respects a diversity of emotional expressions without automatically resorting to pathologization (Riddell, 2012).

In summary, the voices of dissent against the medicalization
of hysteria illuminate the multifaceted challenges posed by this
approach. These critiques advocate for a reevaluation of our understanding of emotional distress, urging a shift toward more nuanced, gender-sensitive, and culturally aware strategies that prioritize empowerment, compassion, and authentic holistic well-being
for individuals.

Cultural Reflections: Literature and Media on Medicalized Hysteria

Cultural representations of medicalized hysteria have been pervasive, influencing societal attitudes and shaping collective understanding (Risse, 1988). Literature and media have played a
significant role in both perpetuating and challenging the medicalization of female emotions. Historically, literature has often
depicted the pathologization of women's emotional experiences,

reinforcing stereotypes while stigmatizing those displaying symptoms associated with hysteria. Yet, within this literary landscape exists a counter-narrative where authors expose the damaging consequences of medicalization and illuminate the intricate realities of women's psychological well-being.

This dialectical relationship between literature and medicalized hysteria reflects the ongoing struggle to dismantle ingrained biases and misconceptions regarding women's mental health (Layne, 2019). In the realm of media, portrayals of medicalized hysteria have varied widely, from sensationalized dramatizations to poignant critiques of the medical establishment. Films, television shows, and documentaries often oscillate between perpetuating harmful tropes and offering platforms for advocacy and education.

The intersection of literature and media in the portrayal of medicalized hysteria underscores the enduring influence of societal attitudes and the formidable power of storytelling in shaping public discourse. As we navigate the intricate interplay between cultural narratives and mental health, we must critically engage with these representations, acknowledging their potential to reinforce damaging myths while simultaneously challenging dominant paradigms. Thus, examining cultural reflections on medicalized hysteria transcends mere literary and cinematic analysis; it becomes an ethical and social inquiry into how our beliefs and values are constructed and disseminated.

Patient Narratives: Lived Experiences of Women Diagnosed with Hysteria

Throughout history, women have frequently found themselves as subjects of hysteria diagnoses, and their lived experiences offer invaluable insights into the repercussions of medicalization on mental health (Ussher, 2013). Such narratives reveal the profound psychological and social consequences of being labeled as 'hysterical,' exposing the trauma that ensues from stigmatization and misunderstanding within medical contexts.

Many of these patient stories illustrate the disconcerting effects of misdiagnosis and the resultant treatment protocols that disregard the nuances of individual emotional experiences. For instance, women have often reported feelings of alienation and frustration as their real struggles are overshadowed by societal prejudices that diminish their emotional complexities (Tasca et al., 2012). The narrative of a woman subjected to invasive procedures, based on the erroneous belief that her emotional distress was purely somatic, highlights the historical ethos dictating medical responses to female patients.

These testimonies not only accentuate the need for reform in how women's psychological health is assessed and treated but also serve as critical reminders of the importance of listening to and validating patient experiences. By amplifying these voices, we cultivate a more profound understanding of the implications that hysterical diagnoses have on women's lives, advocating for a systemic shift in how mental health care is conceived and delivered (Riddell, 2012).

Reassessing Medicalization: Toward a More Nuanced Understanding

Recent years have witnessed a burgeoning recognition of the limitations and harms inflicted by the medicalization of women's emotions, particularly concerning the historical diagnosis of hysteria. Contemporary perspectives on mental health increasingly underscore the necessity to reassess the medicalization framework, directing our focus toward a more nuanced understanding that contemplates the multifaceted interplay of biological, psychological, and social factors underpinning emotional distress (Alves, 2020).

A central tenet of this reassessment is the acknowledgment of diverse cultural and societal influences that shape individuals' emotional experiences. By situating emotional distress within this broader context, we can move beyond a strictly medical interpretation, recognizing the vital role of sociocultural norms and expectations in shaping emotional responses (Weitz, 2004).

Furthermore, this reevaluation emphasizes the importance of involving patients as active participants in their care. Collaborative decision-making and patient-centric approaches proffer a more holistic view of emotional well-being, empowering individuals to engage meaningfully in their treatment trajectories (Riddell, 2012). A more nuanced comprehension of mental health also necessitates a thorough reexamination of diagnostic criteria and treatment protocols. Rather than relying exclusively on rigid medical frameworks, there is a compelling need to embrace interdisciplinary perspectives that integrate psychological, social, and neurobiological dimensions (Hooper, 2019). Such an approach aims to tailor interventions to individual requirements, honoring the unique experiences and expressions of emotional distress encountered across diverse demographics.

Additionally, this reassessment demands careful scrutiny of the pharmaceutical interventions that have historically underpinned the medicalization of hysteria. While recognizing the potential benefits of pharmacotherapy, it is crucial to balance medication with alternative therapeutic avenues, including psychotherapy, mindfulness practices, and lifestyle modifications (Pathiraja et al., 2022). This multifaceted strategy affirms the complexity of emotional suffering while avoiding an overreliance on medication as a standardized solution for all.

In conclusion, the reassessment of medicalization endeavors to cultivate a balanced and inclusive understanding of emotional distress, steering away from reductionist biomedical models. By embracing the human experience's multidimensional nature, we can work toward more compassionate, person-centered, and culturally attuned strategies for supporting individuals grappling with emotional challenges.

In a Nutshell:

Medicalization of Hysteria: Pathologizing Women's Emotions

The medicalization of hysteria has a long history, deeply intertwined with cultural and medical discourses that pathologize women's emotions. This phenomenon has evolved over centuries, reflecting changing societal attitudes towards women's mental health and emotional expression.

Key Insights

- **Historical Context and Cultural Metaphor**:

    - Hysteria has been historically viewed as a disorder primarily affecting women, with its roots traced back to the second millennium BC. It was often linked to women's bodies and emotions, seen as inherently pathological and incapable of restraint.

    - In literature, such as Henry Fielding's "Joseph Andrews," women's emotional expressions, particularly those of unfulfilled desire, were depicted as hysterical. This portrayal reinforced the cultural metaphor of women's bodies as sites of emotional and existential distress.

- **Scientific and Demonological Perspectives**:

  ○ Over 4000 years, hysteria was interpreted through both scientific and demonological lenses. Treatments ranged from herbal remedies and sexual interventions to punitive measures like fire, reflecting its association with sorcery and, later, clinical disease.

  ○ The transition from demonological to scientific perspectives marked a shift in how hysteria was understood and treated, although outdated methods persisted in some regions well into the 19th century.

- **Evolution and Decline of Hysteria**:

  ○ The 20th century saw a decline in the diagnosis of hysteria in Western societies, attributed to changing social conditions and the influence of Westernization. The disorder's prevalence shifted to non-Western countries, highlighting the role of cultural and societal factors in its manifestation.

  ○ The removal of "hysterical neurosis" from the DSM-III in 1980 signified a significant change in the medical community's approach to diagnosing and understanding hysteria, moving away from gendered and culturally specific interpretations.

Conclusion

The medicalization of hysteria has historically pathologized women's emotions, reflecting broader cultural and societal attitudes. Over time, the understanding and treatment of hysteria have evolved, moving from demonological and punitive approaches to more scientific and clinical perspectives. The decline of hysteria in Western societies and its shift to non-Western contexts underscore the influence of cultural factors on the perception and diagnosis of mental health disorders.

References

Althaus, J. (1866). A Lecture on the Pathology and Treatment of Hysteria. British Medical Journal, 1, 245 - 248. https://doi.org/10.1136/bmj.1.271.245.

Alves, K. (2020). "Whither doth this violent Passion hurry us?": Hysterical Language and Desiring Women in Henry Fielding's Joseph Andrews. Eighteenth-Century Fiction, 32, 559 - 578. https://doi.org/10.3138/ecf.32.4.559.

Hooper, G. (2019). Hysteria: Medicine as a Vehicle for Gendered Social Control. 77–90.

Hooper, G. (2019). Hysteria: Medicine as a Vehicle for Gendered Social Control. , 77-90. https://doi.org/10.25611/BHYN-7Q51.

Lader, M., & Sartorius, N. (1968). Anxiety in patients with hysterical conversion symptoms.. Journal of Neurology, Neurosurgery & Psychiatry, 31, 490 - 495. https://doi.org/10.1136/jnnp.31.5.490.

Layne, M. (2019). A SHORT "HISTORY" OF HYSTERIA. Approaching Hysteria. https://doi.org/10.1515/9780691194486-004.

Oakley, A. (1984). The Captured Womb: A history of the medical care of women in pregnancy. Blackwell Science.

Pathiraja, P., Vanga, A., Paramanathan, P., & Kieser, M. (2022). Should we stop using the term 'hysterectomy'? If yes, then why?. Australian and New Zealand Journal of Obstetrics and Gynaecology, 62. https://doi.org/10.1111/ajo.13554.

Riddell, S. (2012). The medicalization of women's emotional experiences: Hysteria in modern psychiatry. Routledge.

Risse, G. (1988). Hysteria at the Edinburgh Infirmary: the construction and treatment of a disease, 1770-1800.. Medical History, 32, 1 - 22. https://doi.org/10.1017/S0025727300047578.

Tasca, C., Rapetti, M., Carta, M., & Fadda, B. (2012). Women And Hysteria In The History Of Mental Health. Clinical Practice and Epidemiology in Mental Health: CP & EMH, 8, 110 - 119. https://doi.org/10.2174/1745017901208010110.

Ussher, J. (2013). Diagnosing difficult women and pathologising femininity: Gender bias in psychiatric nosology. Feminism & Psychology, 23, 63 - 69. https://doi.org/10.1177/095935351246 7968.

Watkins, E. (2000). The technology of orgasm: "hysteria," the vibrator, and women's sexual satisfaction. The Journal of American History, 87, 244-245. https://doi.org/10.2307/2567990.

Weitz, R. (2004). The sociology of health, illness, and health care: A critical approach. Wadsworth Cengage Learning.

CHAPTER NINE

THE FEMININE EXPERIENCE OF HYSTERIA

The Intricacies of Hysteria Through the Lens of Female Experience

The historical tapestry of hysteria is intricately woven with the narratives of women across epochs. From the archaic notion of the "wandering womb" to the Victorian categorization of "female hysteria," women have markedly occupied the forefront of this perplexing affliction (Briggs, 2000). This examination ventures into the distinctive feminine experiences of hysteria, scrutinizing the societal and cultural currents that have sculpted women's interactions with this multifaceted condition.

Throughout the ages, women's encounters with hysteria have been profoundly influenced by contemporaneous perceptions of gender and femininity. The ancient theory of the "wandering womb" not only insinuated physiological ramifications but also bore substantial cultural and societal implications. The tenet that women's emotional fluctuations were somehow tethered to the erratic motion of their reproductive organs served to legitimize restrictive roles and expectations imposed upon them in archaic societies. This paradigm reinforced the notion that women's primary existence hinged on their reproductive capacity, thereby trivializing their emotional and psychological tribulations as mere reflections of physiological discord (Chodoff, 1982).

As we traverse the medieval and Renaissance eras, the contours of women's experiences of hysteria reveal themselves as further molded by societal constructs and normative expectations concerning feminine comportment. The emergence of witch trials and the ensuing vilification of women exhibiting non-conformity or audacious behavior instigated a pervasive anxiety, detrimentally affecting their mental and emotional health. The rampant persecution of those who diverged from prescriptive gender roles substantially augmented incidents of hysteria, acting as a conduit for expressing their repressed angst and trepidation (Zaviršek, 2000).

The 19th century heralded a pivotal transformation in the understanding and medical characterization of female hysteria. The Victorian epoch witnessed an unprecedented rise in diagnoses, as medical practitioners attributed their manifestations to intrinsic nervosity and emotional fragility (Lerner, 1974). The inception of the infamous "hysterical paroxysm," an ostensibly clinical term encapsulating the medicalization of women's sexual experiences, further entrenched the pathologization of female sexuality and the expression of emotions (Showalter, 1997). This period solidified an inflection point in the medical interpretation of women's experiences, firmly embedding the perception of female susceptibility and instability within both medical and societal discourses.

Moreover, the predominance of male-dominated medical paradigms in the 19th century engendered a myopic and biased comprehension of female physiology and psychology (Showalter, 1997). The systematic exclusion of women from both medical education and research perpetuated the simplification of women's physiological and psychological intricacies, relegating them to the realms of hysteria and emotional tumult (Farina, 2016). While the advent of psychoanalysis by luminaries such as Sigmund Freud and Jean-Martin Charcot represented groundbreaking advancements, it simultaneously reinforced the association of femininity with hysteria, perpetuating the notion that women's emotional and psychological experiences were innately pathological (Kohon, 2017).

Contemporary societal attitudes and gender norms continue to shape the feminine experience of hysteria. Despite notable advancements in women's rights and autonomy, prevailing societal pressures and expectations incessantly influence women's mental and emotional well-being (Schaeffer, 2014). The shifting paradigms of gender expectations, alongside the persistent scourge of gender-based violence and discrimination, engender ongoing tribulations for women's mental health (Mancini et al., 2022). The intersectionality of gender, race, and socioeconomic realities complicates the feminine experience, as women from marginalized backgrounds often confront distinct barriers in accessing crucial mental health resources (Tasca et al., 2012).

To truly comprehend the feminine experience of hysteria, one must acknowledge the multifaceted nature of women's mental health challenges and the imperative for holistic, intersectional approaches in addressing these concerns (Bartleet, 2013). Recognizing the historical, cultural, and societal influences that have shaped women's encounters with hysteria can pave the way toward fostering a more compassionate, inclusive, and equitable society—one that genuinely values and nurtures women's emotional and psychological welfare.

The intricate interrelations between hormonal fluctuations, societal stressors, and expectations further obfuscate the understanding of hysteria in women. The menstrual cycle has long been correlated with emotional and physical variability, often to the detriment of women's mental health (McLaren, 1999). Stress—a

prevalent catalyst for hysteria—interacts with hormonal variations, establishing a cyclical dynamic that can intensify symptoms. Additionally, societal imperatives dictating that women
embody nurturing, compliant, and emotionally steadfast per-
sonas exacerbate the existential burdens they bear, compelling
them to suppress their authentic emotional experiences, thus
manifesting psychological distress through the prism of hysteria.

Exploring Trauma and Hysteria: The Feminine Experience

The profound implications of trauma, especially gender-based
violence, and historical oppression demand critical consideration when dissecting the feminine experience of hysteria (Lutz,
2013). Women subjected to sexual assault, domestic abuse,
or systemic discrimination exhibit a significantly heightened
propensity for developing hysterical symptoms, as these traumatic experiences exact a severe psychological and emotional toll (Mancini et al., 2022). Compounding this issue is the
intergenerational transmission of trauma; women from marginalized communities may bear the collective agony of their
ancestors, engendering an amplified vulnerability to hysteria
and associated psychological illnesses (Tasca et al., 2012).

The professional and societal response to women's displays of
distress and emotional upheaval has fundamentally shaped the
feminine experience of hysteria. Historically, women manifesting
symptoms of hysteria have frequently been marginalized, pathologized, or even subjected to invasive and often harmful medical
interventions (Showalter, 1997). This reflects a pervasive pattern
of gendered discrimination entrenched within the healthcare system. The longstanding belief in women's intrinsic irrationality and
weakness has trivialized their emotional and psychological strug-

gles, exacerbating their suffering and obstructing their access to timely and effective mental health care (Farina, 2016).

A thorough examination of the feminine experience of hysteria reveals that a holistic understanding of women's mental health necessitates an exploration of the intricate interplay of biological, psychological, social, and cultural influences (Lutz, 2013). By unraveling this complex tapestry of factors that contribute to women's experiences of hysteria, we can foster greater empathy, awareness, and advocacy for the diverse spectrum of mental health needs that women encounter. Initiatives aimed at dismantling antiquated gender norms, expanding access to mental health services, and prioritizing trauma-informed care are imperative for forging a future where women's experiences of hysteria are acknowledged with understanding, validation, and support.

To fully comprehend the feminine experience of hysteria, it is critical to explore the psychological and emotional burdens imposed by societal expectations and gender-based discrimination. The relentless pressure to conform to idealized standards of femininity, coupled with the disproportionate share of caregiving and emotional labor allocated to women, cultivates chronic stress and emotional suppression, which may ultimately manifest as hysteria (Schaeffer, 2014). The societal imperative for women to serve as nurturers and caretakers while neglecting their own mental wellness further entrenches their susceptibility to emotional distress and psychological difficulties (Zaviršek, 2000).

The term "hysteria" has historically functioned as a tool to delegitimize and dismiss women's legitimate emotional and psychological experiences, perpetuating the notion that their distress stems solely from inherent emotional volatility (Briggs, 2000). This pervasive stereotype undermines the authenticity of women's emotions, hindering their capacity to seek and receive appropriate support and treatment for their mental health challenges. The association of hysteria with the feminine experience has fostered a detrimental cycle of stigma and trivialization, obstructing women's agency in addressing their emotional and psychological well-being (Lerner, 1974).

Moreover, the diverse experiences of women across varying cultural and socioeconomic landscapes intersect significantly with their encounters with hysteria. Those from marginalized backgrounds face compounded barriers in accessing adequate mental health care, grappling with systemic obstacles such as the lack of culturally sensitive resources, linguistic limitations, and economic disparities (Tasca et al., 2012). The historical trauma and ongoing discrimination faced by these women contribute to elevated levels of psychological distress, further amplifying their susceptibility to hysteria and related mental health conditions (Chodoff, 1982).

Additionally, the intersection of race and gender infuses yet another layer of complexity into the feminine experience of hysteria. Women of color are frequently subjected to unique forms of discrimination and marginalization, profoundly influencing their encounters with mental health challenges (Zaviršek, 2000). This intersectional impact markedly underscores the urgency for recognizing and addressing the diverse needs of women across various racial and ethnic backgrounds, thereby ensuring that interventions are truly inclusive and responsive to their multifaceted experiences.

In conclusion, addressing the feminine experience of hysteria through the prism of trauma allows for a richer, more nuanced understanding of the psychological struggles women face. Recognizing the intricate relationships between historical oppression, societal expectations, and the ongoing impacts of trauma is essential for fostering a supportive environment that validates women's experiences and promotes their emotional and psychological health (Farina, 2016).

The Impact of Historical Trauma and Identity on Hysteria Among Women of Color

The enduring aftermath of colonialism, racism, and systemic oppression has indelibly shaped the mental health landscape for women of color, heightening their susceptibility to mental health disorders such as hysteria (Showalter, 1997). The intergenerational transmission of trauma, coupled with the systematic erasure of their narratives within dominant cultural discourses, amplifies the psychological burdens carried by these women. Thus, it becomes imperative to adopt a holistic and culturally nuanced approach to support their mental well-being, acknowledging the unique contexts from which these challenges arise (Lutz, 2013).

A critical aspect of the feminine experience of hysteria is rooted in women's complex relationships with their bodies and sexuality. The incessant objectification and commodification of women's bodies in contemporary media and popular culture contribute to the internalization of shame and guilt surrounding their sexuality (Mancini et al., 2022). This distortion fosters a fragmented and disempowered connection to both their physical and emotional selves. Women often perceive their bodies as sites of vulnerability, leading to self-objectification that exacerbates psychological distress and may manifest as the physical symptoms associated with hysteria (Lerner, 1974).

Moreover, the intersectionality of gender identity with hysteria complicates the feminine experience considerably. Transgender and non-binary individuals, particularly those assigned female at birth, encounter unique challenges in accessing mental health care within a predominantly cisnormative and binary healthcare framework (Chodoff, 1982). The conflation of gender dysphoria, societal discrimination, and psychological turmoil necessitates a more inclusive and affirming approach to understanding and supporting the mental health needs of gender-diverse individuals, highlighting the inadequacies of traditional frameworks that fail to account for their lived experiences.

As the experiences of women regarding hysteria evolve in our rapidly changing global context, it is crucial to amplify their voices and diversify the narratives surrounding mental health. By validating and elevating the experiences of women from varied backgrounds, we can cultivate a broader and more empathetic understanding of hysteria and related psychological conditions (McLaren, 1999). Implementing culturally responsive mental health care, trauma-informed interventions, and the destigmatization of emotional expression are essential for promoting mental health equity and empowerment across all identities and lived experiences.

In conclusion, the feminine experience of hysteria is intricately intertwined with the historical, cultural, and societal frameworks that have shaped women's mental and emotional well-being (Showalter, 1997). A comprehensive understanding of the factors influencing women's encounters with hysteria must take into account the multifaceted influences of gender, race, sexuality, trauma, and gender identity. Advocating for a paradigm shift in women's mental health approach is essential—one that emphasizes the intersectional nature of women's experiences and prioritizes inclusive, empathetic, and empowering responses to their emotional and psychological needs (Farina, 2016).

By undertaking collective efforts to dismantle gender-based discrimination, increasing access to culturally relevant mental health resources, and elevating the voices of women from marginalized communities, we can forge a future where women's experiences of hysteria are met with compassion, understanding, and holistic support (Tasca et al., 2012).

In a Nutshell:

The Feminine Experience of Hysteria

Hysteria has historically been closely associated with women, often seen as a distinctly feminine disorder. This association has evolved over time, influenced by cultural, social, and medical perspectives. The following synthesis presents key insights from various research papers on the feminine experience of hysteria.

Key Insights

- **Historical and Cultural Context**:

    - Hysteria has been considered a female disease for millennia, with treatments ranging from herbal remedies to punitive measures, reflecting its deep cultural and historical roots.

    - The diagnosis of hysteria has been predominantly applied to women, often reflecting societal and cultural pressures rather than purely medical conditions.

- **Psychoanalytic Perspectives**:

    - Hysteria is linked to the development of femininity, with psychoanalytic theories suggesting it arises from unresolved oedipal conflicts and the struggle to define sexual identity.

    - The concept of hysteria has evolved within psychoanalytic theory, with early cases like Dora's highlighting the role of transference and the complexities of female sexual identity.

- **Feminist Critiques**:

  - Feminist scholars argue that hysteria has been used to control and marginalize women, labeling them as mad to reinforce patriarchal norms.

  - The association of hysteria with femininity is seen as a caricature, influenced by male-dominated cultural forces rather than inherent female traits.

- **Modern Interpretations**:

  - Contemporary views suggest that hysteria is not exclusively a female disorder but a universal condition manifesting in various forms, such as chronic fatigue syndrome and Gulf War syndrome.

  - The modern understanding of hysteria involves recognizing it as a complex interplay of psychological, social, and cultural factors rather than a simple gendered pathology.

- **Artistic and Literary Representations**:

  - Artistic practices and feminist literature have reinterpreted hysteria, viewing it as a form of resistance against the social construction of sexual roles and identities.

  - Women artists and writers have used hysteria as a metaphor to explore and challenge the limitations imposed by patriarchal society.

Conclusion

The feminine experience of hysteria is deeply intertwined with cultural, social, and historical contexts. While traditionally seen as a female disorder, modern interpretations recognize it as a complex condition influenced by various factors. Feminist critiques highlight the role of hysteria in reinforcing gender norms, while contemporary views and artistic representations offer new ways of understanding and challenging this association.

References

Bartleet, C. (2013). Sarah Daniels' Hysteria Plays: Re-presentations of Madness in Ripen Our Darkness and Head-Rot Holiday. Modern Drama, 46, 241 - 260. https://doi.org/10.1353/mdr.20 03.0049.

Briggs, L. (2000). The Race of Hysteria: "Overcivilization" and the "Savage" Woman in Late Nineteenth-Century Obstetrics and Gynecology. American Quarterly, 52, 246 - 273. https://doi.org/ 10.1353/AQ.2000.0013.

Chodoff, P. (1982). Hysteria and women.. The American journal of psychiatry, 139 5, 545-51 . https://doi.org/10.1176/AJP.1 39.5.545.

Farina, M. (2016). Hysteria and the feminine: The intersection of psychology and gender. Transformations Press.

Kohon, G. (2017). Reflections on Dora: the case of hysteria.. The International journal of psycho-analysis, 65 (Pt 1), 73-84. https://doi.org/10.4324/9781351262880-22.

Lerner, H. (1974). The hysterical personality: a "woman's disease".. Comprehensive psychiatry, 15 2, 157-64 . https://doi.org/ 10.1016/0010-440X(74)90032-7.

Lutz, A. (2013). The embodiment of emotion: A feminist perspective on hysteria. University of Iowa Press.

Mancini, M., Scudiero, M., Mignogna, S., Urso, V., & Stanghellini, G. (2022). Se-duction is not sex-duction: Desexualizing and de-feminizing hysteria. Frontiers in Psychology, 13. https://doi.org/10.3389/fpsyg.2022.963117.

McLaren, R. (1999). The Discourses of Hysteria: Menopause, Art and the Body. Hecate, 25, 107.

Schaeffer, J. (2014). Hysteria: The Feminine Risk. Figures De La Psychanalyse, 55-67.

Showalter, E. (1997). Hystories: Hysterical Epidemics and Modern Culture. . https://doi.org/10.5860/choice.35-0946.

Showalter, E. (1997). The female malady: Women, madness, and English culture, 1830-1980. Virago Press.

Tasca, C., Rapetti, M., Carta, M., & Fadda, B. (2012). Women And Hysteria In The History Of Mental Health. Clinical Practice and Epidemiology in Mental Health: CP & EMH, 8, 110 - 119. https://doi.org/10.2174/1745017901208010110.

Zaviršek, D. (2000). A Historical Overview of Women's Hysteria in Slovenia. European Journal of Women's Studies, 7, 169–188.

CHAPTER TEN

THE CONTEMPORARY UNDERSTANDING OF RELATED MENTAL HEALTH DISORDERS

Modern Diagnostic Frameworks in Psychiatry

The evolution of modern psychiatry has profoundly transformed diagnostic paradigms, effectively supplanting the antiquated notion of hysteria. Central to this advancement are the Diagnostic and Statistical Manual of Mental Disorders (DSM) (American Psychiatric Association, 2013) and the International Classification of Diseases (ICD), which serve as foundational tools for the categorization and classification of mental health conditions. These frameworks provide a standardized lexicon for clinicians, researchers, and policymakers, thereby facilitating a collective approach to identifying, diagnosing, and treating mental health disorders.

Transition from Hysteria to Empirical Diagnoses

The shift from the nebulous classification of hysteria to well-defined diagnoses such as anxiety disorders, depression, and post-traumatic stress disorder (PTSD) marks a pivotal development in psychiatric practice (Jacob, Patel, & Patel, 2014). This transformation reflects an increasing recognition of the nuanced expressions of psychological distress and the necessity for precise, evidence-based diagnostic criteria that consider a range of symptomatology and underlying causes (Chapman, Perry, & Strine, 2004). In its various iterations, the DSM has significantly influenced contemporary psychiatry by delineating specific diagnostic criteria and guidelines across diverse mental health conditions. This approach entails a comprehensive assessment that evaluates symptomatology, duration, and functional impairment, thus underscoring the importance of an integrated evaluation that encompasses biological, psychological, and social dimensions (Fried et al., 2016). Complementarily, the ICD, established by the World Health Organization (WHO), affords a global lens on mental health diagnostics, thus harmonizing practices across different cultural contexts (Clark et al., 2017).

Continuous Revision and Improvement

A hallmark of these modern diagnostic frameworks is their commitment to ongoing revision in response to the latest empirical research and clinical findings. This adaptability allows for classifications that reflect current knowledge and the evolving needs of healthcare providers and their patients (Gómez-Carrillo & Kirmayer, 2023). Importantly, the frameworks advocate for differential diagnoses, acknowledging the complex nature of mental health presentations and striving to avoid the pitfalls of misdiagnosis and overgeneralization (Hofmann, Curtiss, & McNally,

2016). As we advance our understanding of mental health disorders, it is essential to recognize how these contemporary diagnostic frameworks have redefined the conceptualization of psychological distress. They have transitioned the field from vague, stigmatized labels such as hysteria toward precise, evidence-based classifications that enhance assessment accuracy, treatment planning, and outcomes for individuals facing mental health challenges.

Post-Hysteria Diagnoses: Anxiety Disorders, Depression, and PTSD

The evolution from the historical concept of hysteria into contemporary diagnostic categories has yielded profound insights into mental health disorders. In the wake of the hysteria paradigm, medical professionals have strived to articulate specific conditions that were previously encapsulated under the expansive label of hysteria. Among the most prominent post-hysteria diagnoses are anxiety disorders, depression, and post-traumatic stress disorder (PTSD).

Anxiety Disorders

Anxiety disorders encompass a broad array of conditions, including generalized anxiety disorder, panic disorder, social anxiety disorder, and specific phobias. These disorders are characterized by excessive worry, fear, and apprehension, profoundly impacting individuals' daily functioning and overall quality of life. The delineation and recognition of these disorders have enabled the development of targeted interventions, ranging from cognitive-behavioral therapies to pharmacological treatments, thereby addressing specific manifestations of anxiety (Zinbarg, Williams, & Mineka, 2022).

Depression

Often referred to as the "common cold" of mental illness, depression holds a prominent place as a prevalent diagnosis with extensive ramifications. It includes various subtypes, such as major depressive disorder, persistent depressive disorder, and disruptive mood dysregulation disorder. Contemporary understandings of depression extend beyond merely melancholic moods to embrace a complex interplay of biological, psychological, and environmental factors (Mineka & Zinbarg, 2006). Treatment modalities, including antidepressant medications and psychotherapeutic approaches, target symptom alleviation and recovery from the multifaceted nature of depression.

Post-Traumatic Stress Disorder (PTSD)

PTSD has emerged as a significant acknowledgment of the enduring effects of trauma on psychological well-being. Traditionally associated with experiences such as military combat, natural disasters, or interpersonal violence, PTSD comprises a constellation of symptoms, including intrusive memories, hypervigilance, and emotional numbness (Wilson, 2019). Research into the neurobiological foundations of PTSD has advanced trauma-focused therapies, leading to treatment methodologies such as eye movement desensitization and reprocessing (EMDR) and prolonged exposure therapy (Taylor, 2015).

Conclusion: Towards Enhanced Understanding and Treatment

As we stand at the crossroads of hysteria's legacy and contemporary psychiatric discourse, an incisive examination of anxiety disorders, depression, and PTSD underscores the necessity for refining diagnostic frameworks and implementing tailored treatment strategies. Through continued research efforts and clinical innovations, the transition from hysteria to these precise diagnoses illuminates the evolving landscape of mental health understanding and care.

The Role of Trauma in Present-Day Psychological Health

Recent decades have sparked a paradigm shift in our comprehension and treatment of mental health disorders, revealing the pervasive influence of trauma in psychological well-being. Trauma arising from acute incidents such as accidents or violent acts or from chronic experiences such as abuse or neglect is recognized as a crucial factor contributing to the development of various mental health conditions (Rajabzadeh et al., 2021). The concept of PTSD has drawn significant attention, highlighting the long-lasting consequences of trauma on individual health.

Trauma's Intricate Relationship with Mental Health Conditions

Research has elucidated the intricate connections between trauma and the onset of conditions such as anxiety disorders and depression. Individuals exposed to traumatic experiences often report heightened anxiety, flashbacks, nightmares, and other symptoms emblematic of PTSD (Fried et al., 2016). Moreover, the emotional ramifications of trauma can present as persistent feelings of sadness, hopelessness, and a disinterest in previously enjoyed activities, aligning with the diagnostic criteria for major depressive disorder (Clark et al., 2017). A nuanced understanding of how trauma interplays with these prevalent mental health conditions is essential for effective assessment and intervention.

Gendered Impact of Trauma

It is critical to acknowledge that the ramifications of trauma are often gendered, with notable differences in the prevalence and expression of trauma-related disorders between genders (Gómez-Carrillo & Kirmayer, 2023). Research consistently indicates that women are more susceptible to developing PTSD, anxiety, and depression following exposure to trauma, underscoring the need for gender-sensitive approaches in clinical practice (Jacob, Patel, & Patel, 2014). Societal factors, including gender-based violence and systemic inequities, further contribute to the varied experiences of trauma and subsequent mental health outcomes among diverse gender identities.

Neurobiological Insights into Trauma

Contemporary psychiatric discussions have also illuminated the neurobiological foundations of trauma's influence on psychological health. Investigations have revealed alterations in brain structure and function associated with trauma, particularly in areas linked to emotional regulation and stress response (Fried et al., 2016). These findings emphasize the intricate interplay between biological and environmental elements in shaping an individual's vulnerability to mental health challenges following trauma exposure.

Path Forward: Comprehensive Trauma-Informed Care

A multifaceted approach encompassing assessment, treatment, and advocacy is essential to facilitating a comprehensive understanding of trauma in contemporary psychological health. Integrating principles of trauma-informed care into clinical practice, promoting resilience-building strategies, and advocating for systemic changes to alleviate the societal roots of trauma are vital endeavors in mitigating trauma's profound impact on mental well-being (Hofmann, Curtiss, & McNally, 2016).

Gender Differences in Mental Health Outcomes

In modern mental health discourse, exploring gender differences in mental health outcomes has emerged as a pivotal area of inquiry. Understanding how mental health conditions present differently across genders has significant implications for clinical practice, research, and public health policies (Hofmann, Curtiss, & McNally, 2016). Evidence suggests that gender influences the prevalence, manifestation, and treatment responses of various mental health disorders.

Internalizing vs. Externalizing Disorders

For instance, studies have demonstrated that women are more prone to experience internalizing disorders such as depression and anxiety, while men exhibit higher rates of externalizing conditions, including substance use disorders and antisocial behaviors (Rajabzadeh et al., 2021). Additionally, societal gender norms and expectations can shape help-seeking behaviors and symptom expression, further complicating the landscape of gender-specific mental health outcomes.

Interplay of Biological, Psychological, and Social Factors

Analyzing gender differences in mental health outcomes necessitates consideration of biological, psychological, and social influences. Biological factors, including hormonal fluctuations and genetic susceptibilities, may account for variations in the prevalence and presentation of certain mental health conditions (Zinbarg, Williams, & Mineka, 2022). Concurrently, psychological theories suggest that socialization and cultural factors influence gender-specific coping mechanisms, emotional regulation strategies, and responses to stress, thus highlighting the need for an intersectional approach that incorporates considerations of gender, race, socioeconomic status, and other identity factors in examining mental health outcomes.

Tailoring Treatment Approaches

From a therapeutic perspective, recognizing the gender-specific manifestations of mental health conditions is crucial for delivering equitable and effective care. Crafting treatment strategies tailored to acknowledge gender-related nuances in symptomatology and underlying mechanisms can enhance the relevance and precision of interventions (Zinbarg, Williams, & Mineka, 2022). Moreover, addressing systemic inequities and entrenched gender stereotypes is vital for promoting inclusive and accessible mental health support for individuals of all gender identities.

Future Research Directions

As research continues to delve into the complex intersections of gender and mental health, fostering multidisciplinary collaborations and amplifying diverse voices within this field will be essential. Such efforts will advance our understanding and enable more targeted responses to individuals navigating mental health challenges' unique needs (Clark et al., 2017).

Neuroscience Perspectives on Emotional Dysregulation

Emotional dysregulation is a complex phenomenon that has garnered extensive attention in neuroscience and mental health research. At its essence, emotional dysregulation refers to the inability to effectively manage or modulate emotional responses, often resulting in heightened reactivity, impulsivity, and challenges in coping with everyday stressors.

Neural Underpinnings of Emotional Dysregulation

Recent advancements in neuroimaging techniques, such as functional magnetic resonance imaging (fMRI) and electroencephalography (EEG), have revealed irregularities in key brain regions associated with emotion regulation among individuals experiencing emotional dysregulation (Hofmann, Curtiss, & McNally, 2016). The amygdala, a critical center for processing emotional stimuli, often exhibits hyperactivity in these individuals, contributing to exaggerated fear responses and increased emotional arousal. Additionally, dysfunctions in the prefrontal cortex, responsible for cognitive control and emotion regulation, have been linked to difficulties in managing affective states.

Neurochemical Factors

Moreover, research into neurotransmitter systems, particularly serotonin and dopamine, has highlighted the impact of neurochemical imbalances on emotional functioning. Dysregulated serotonin levels have been associated with mood instability and impulsive behaviors, while alterations in dopamine signaling may lead to heightened reward-seeking behaviors and disrupted emotional processing (Fried et al., 2016). These neurochemical fluctuations not only exacerbate emotional dysregulation but also interact with various psychiatric disorders, including depression, anxiety, and personality disorders.

Innovative Intervention Strategies

Neuroscience insights have facilitated the development of novel intervention strategies to address emotional dysregulation. Neurofeedback, a therapeutic method grounded in operant conditioning principles, allows individuals to modulate their brain activity by receiving real-time feedback on their neural patterns (Zinbarg, Williams, & Mineka, 2022). Additionally, pharmacological approaches aimed at restoring neurochemical equilibrium and modulating neural circuitry are being explored as potential interventions for emotional dysregulation.

Future Directions in Assessment and Treatment

As our understanding of the neural substrates underlying emotional dysregulation progresses, interdisciplinary collaboration among neuroscientists, clinicians, and mental health practitioners offers promise for creating personalized and effective interventions. By integrating neurobiological perspectives with clinical observations, we can pave the way for advancements in the assessment, diagnosis, and treatment of emotional dysregulation, ultimately enhancing the well-being of individuals grappling with these pervasive issues.

Psychological Theories and Models of Affective Disorders

In the domain of mental health, affective disorders encompass a broad range of conditions characterized by disturbances in mood and emotional regulation. As we traverse this intricate landscape, it is imperative to explore the diverse psychological theories and models that enrich our understanding of these complex conditions.

The Biopsychosocial Model

One prominent framework is the Biopsychosocial Model, which posits that an individual's mental well-being is shaped by the interplay of biological, psychological, and social factors (Clark et al., 2017). This holistic approach recognizes the intricate web of influences contributing to affective disorders, guiding clinicians toward multifaceted and integrated intervention strategies.

Cognitive Theories: Cognitive Behavioral Therapy

Cognitive theories, particularly Cognitive Behavioral Therapy (CBT), have significantly transformed our comprehension and treatment of affective disorders (Hofmann, Curtiss, & McNally, 2016). CBT emphasizes the pivotal role of maladaptive thought patterns and behaviors in perpetuating emotional distress. This therapeutic approach empowers individuals to challenge and reframe their cognitive processes, fostering adaptive coping strategies and restructuring negative beliefs. As such, CBT has emerged as a cornerstone in the therapeutic arsenal for addressing affective disorders.

Attachment Theory
Attachment theory further elucidates the development and manifestation of affective disorders. Pioneered by John Bowlby, this theory underscores the critical role of early interpersonal relationships in shaping emotional regulation (Taylor, 2015). By comprehending various attachment styles, clinicians gain valuable insights into how relational dynamics influence affective disorders, thereby facilitating targeted interventions that address attachment-related issues.

The Diathesis-Stress Model
Another influential model is the Diathesis-Stress Model, which posits that a genetic predisposition (diathesis) interacts with environmental stressors to precipitate affective disorders (Mineka & Zinbarg, 2006). This conceptual framework elucidates the complex relationship between vulnerability factors and life stressors, thereby illuminating potential etiological pathways. Interventions based on this model aim to identify and mitigate stressors while bolstering resilience, thereby reducing the risk of developing or exacerbating affective disorders.

Psychodynamic Perspectives

Psychodynamic perspectives provide additional depth to our understanding of affective disorders by examining unconscious conflicts and early developmental experiences that shape emotional well-being. Both Freudian and Jungian traditions contribute to our comprehension of the intrapsychic mechanisms underlying affective disorders, enriching therapeutic approaches with insights into unconscious processes and the symbolic representation of affective experiences (Fried et al., 2016).

Integrative Approaches to Understanding Affective Disorders

As we navigate this rich array of psychological theories and models, it becomes evident that a comprehensive understanding of affective disorders necessitates an integrative and multidimensional approach. By synthesizing biological, psychological, and sociocultural perspectives, clinicians and researchers can cultivate nuanced interventions that honor the intricate interplay of factors influencing affective disorders (Jacob, Patel, & Patel, 2014). Ultimately, this holistic framework empowers us to devise personalized and effective strategies to foster resilience and promote emotional well-being for individuals grappling with the complexities of affective disorders.

Therapeutic Interventions: From Psychoanalysis to Cognitive Behavioral Therapy

Exploring therapeutic interventions for affective disorders reveals a historical evolution of treatment modalities that have shaped modern mental health care. Beginning with Sigmund Freud's foundational work in psychoanalysis, this approach aimed to uncover unconscious conflicts through deep discourse between therapist and client. By bringing repressed emotions and childhood experiences into conscious awareness, psychoanalysis paved the way for healing. While its influence endures, the advent of Cognitive Behavioral Therapy (CBT) marked a significant paradigm shift (Hofmann, Curtiss, & McNally, 2016).

Cognitive Behavioral Therapy (CBT)

CBT operates on the principle that thoughts, feelings, and behaviors are interconnected. By identifying and challenging maladaptive thought patterns, individuals can effect meaningful changes in their emotional states (Wilson, 2019). Additionally, incorporating behavioral techniques empowers individuals to confront and modify detrimental actions or responses, ultimately cultivating adaptive coping mechanisms. The versatility of CBT has led to its application across a spectrum of affective disorders, including anxiety, depression, and PTSD, establishing it as a cornerstone of contemporary therapeutic practice.

Mindfulness-Based Interventions

Furthermore, integrating mindfulness-based interventions has garnered considerable attention in recent years. Incorporating techniques such as meditation, breathwork, and body awareness, these approaches provide individuals with tools to cultivate present-moment awareness and develop non-judgmental acceptance of their experiences (Taylor, 2015). This transformative process fosters resilience, self-compassion, and emotional regulation, serving as a powerful adjunct to traditional therapeutic methods.

Dialectical Behavior Therapy (DBT) and Acceptance and Commitment Therapy (ACT)

Additional modalities, including Dialectical Behavior Therapy (DBT) and Acceptance and Commitment Therapy (ACT), offer unique perspectives and techniques that cater to the multifaceted nature of affective disorders. DBT is particularly effective for those struggling with emotion regulation and interpersonal effectiveness, while ACT empowers individuals to accept their thoughts and feelings as part of the human experience (Zinbarg, Williams, & Mineka, 2022).

Personalized and Holistic Care

As mental health professionals refine and expand therapeutic modalities, it is essential to provide personalized care that aligns with each individual's unique needs. The amalgamation of evidence-based practices, clinical expertise, and collaborative engagement forms the bedrock of state-of-the-art mental health care, embodying the commitment to profound healing and sustainable well-being.

Narratives of Recovery: Personal Accounts and Clinical Insights

Recovery from mental health disorders is an intensely personal journey often marked by perseverance, resilience, and the essential support of healthcare professionals and loved ones. This section delves into the narratives of individuals who have traversed the challenges of mental illness and have found pathways to healing and renewal. Through intimate personal accounts, readers gain insight into the diverse experiences of those confronting conditions like anxiety disorders, depression, and PTSD.

The Multifaceted Nature of Recovery

These narratives illuminate the emotional and psychological toll of these conditions while underscoring the intricate nature of recovery. They emphasize the significance of individualized treatment approaches and holistic support systems tailored to each person's needs.

Clinical Insights and Case Studies

In parallel with firsthand stories, this section integrates valuable clinical insights from mental health professionals who have guided patients through their recovery journeys. By merging personal narratives with professional expertise, readers understand the challenges and victories inherent in the recovery process. Detailed case studies further illustrate the nuanced dynamics of mental health treatment, showcasing diverse strategies and modalities employed to facilitate healing and growth (Rajabzadeh et al., 2021).

Advocacy and Destigmatization

Moreover, this exploration highlights the crucial role of advocacy and destigmatization in improving mental health care accessibility and dismantling barriers to treatment. It stresses the necessity for societal attitudinal shifts and systemic reforms prioritizing mental health equity and inclusivity.

This section aims to illuminate the complex landscape of recovery from mental health disorders through the amalgamation of personal narratives and clinical insights. It presents readers with a compelling portrayal of resilience, community support, and the transformative potential of effective intervention.

Societal Attitudes and Accessibility to Mental Health Care

In recent decades, societal attitudes toward mental health have undergone significant transformation, with increasing emphasis on destigmatization and awareness. Yet, despite these advancements, individuals still encounter pervasive misconceptions and discrimination regarding mental illness (Gómez-Carrillo & Kirmayer, 2023). In many cultures, the stigma associated with mental health issues can obstruct individuals from seeking help, engendering a cycle of silence and isolation that exacerbates the impact of mental health disorders.

The Critical Issue of Accessibility

Furthermore, accessibility to mental health care remains a pressing concern, particularly for marginalized communities and underserved populations. Disparities in access to affordable, quality mental health services continue to contribute to unequal health outcomes and intensify existing social inequalities (Chapman, Perry, & Strine, 2004). Addressing these disparities necessitates a multifaceted approach encompassing policy reforms, community outreach, and improved resource allocation.

Integrating Mental Health Services

A vital step toward enhancing accessibility is integrating mental health services into primary care settings (Rajabzadeh et al., 2021). Such integration ensures that individuals can access comprehensive support for their mental well-being. Additionally, expanding telehealth services presents a promising opportunity to bridge geographical barriers, providing vital mental health resources to individuals in remote or isolated areas.

Educational Initiatives

Educational initiatives to raise awareness about mental health, nurture empathy, and promote inclusivity are instrumental in reshaping societal attitudes. By challenging stereotypes and dispelling misconceptions, these initiatives help cultivate a more supportive and understanding environment for those grappling with mental health challenges (Fried et al., 2016).

Collaborative Efforts for Change

Effective collaboration between governmental institutions, healthcare providers, and community organizations is crucial for dismantling barriers to mental health care. We must cultivate a society where individuals feel empowered to seek help without fear of judgment or discrimination. As we navigate the complex landscape of mental health care, advocating for policies and practices that prioritize accessibility, equity, and compassionate support for all individuals facing mental health struggles is imperative (Clark et al., 2017).

Looking Forward: Future Directions in Mental Health Research

As we venture into the future of mental health research, our understanding of mental health disorders continues to evolve rapidly. Several key trends and focus areas are poised to shape the landscape of mental health research in the coming years.

Integrative Perspectives

One such trend is the integration of diverse perspectives within mental health research, embracing interdisciplinary collaboration among fields such as psychology, neuroscience, genetics, and public health (Fried et al., 2016). This integrated approach holds the potential to unravel the complex interplay of biological, psychological, and social factors contributing to mental health disorders.

Personalized Medicine and Precision Psychiatry

A significant area for future exploration lies in personalized medicine and precision psychiatry. Advances in genomics and neuroimaging enable tailored treatment approaches based on individual genetic and neurobiological profiles, thereby enhancing treatment outcomes (Zinbarg, Williams, & Mineka, 2022).

Digital Mental Health Interventions

The rise of digital mental health interventions and telepsychiatry presents an exciting avenue for improving accessibility to mental health care and early intervention, particularly in underserved communities. However, this digital revolution requires rigorous evaluation and refinement to ensure effectiveness and ethical implementation (Hofmann, Curtiss, & McNally, 2016).

Cultural and Global Perspectives

Incorporating cultural and global perspectives into mental health research will be crucial for addressing disparities and providing culturally responsive care (Jacob, Patel, & Patel, 2014). Recognizing the influence of sociocultural determinants on mental health outcomes underscores the need for informed interventions and policies (Gómez-Carrillo & Kirmayer, 2023).

Exploration of the Gut-Brain Axis

Additionally, the ongoing study of the gut-brain axis and its implications for mental health presents novel avenues for research, with the potential for developing innovative therapeutic strategies targeting the microbiome (Zinbarg, Williams, & Mineka, 2022).

Combating Stigma and Promoting Prevention

The mental health research community must also address the persistent challenges posed by stigma and discrimination associated with mental illness, necessitating combined efforts to enhance mental health literacy and promote help-seeking behaviors (Fried et al., 2016). Prioritizing prevention and early intervention through community-based initiatives and public health strategies is essential in light of the increasing prevalence of mental health disorders worldwide.

By aligning research with these future directions, we can foster a more comprehensive and impactful approach to understanding and addressing mental health disorders in the years to come.

In a Nutshell:

Contemporary Understanding of Related Mental Health Disorders

The contemporary understanding of mental health disorders has evolved significantly, incorporating various theoretical frameworks and empirical findings. This synthesis highlights key insights from recent research papers grouped into relevant schools of thought.

Key Insights

- **Learning Theory and Anxiety Disorders**:

  - Contemporary learning theory provides a nuanced understanding of the etiology and maintenance of anxiety disorders, emphasizing the role of early learning histories, temperamental vulnerabilities, and contextual variables during and after stressful events.

- **Global Mental Health (GMH)**:

  - GMH is understood through a conceptual framework that includes research generation, implementation into practice, improving mental health environments, and supporting low-and-middle-income countries (LMICs).

- **Network Theory of Mental Disorders**:

  - Mental disorders can be conceptualized as complex networks of interacting symptoms rather than latent disease entities. This approach helps explain comorbidity, predict treatment outcomes, and suggest novel therapeutic strategies by targeting central symptoms within the network.

- **Classification Systems**:

  ○ The ICD-11, DSM-5, and RDoC provide different frameworks for understanding and classifying mental disorders, each addressing issues like etiology, categorical vs. dimensional phenomena, thresholds, and comorbidity. These systems aim to reduce the burden of mental disorders through improved diagnosis and treatment.

- **Chronic Disease and Depressive Disorders**:

  ○ There is a significant association between depressive disorders and chronic diseases, with each exacerbating the other. This relationship underscores the importance of integrated approaches to managing both mental and physical health.

- **Cultural-Ecosocial Systems View**:

  ○ Mental health problems are influcnced by developmental processes, social contexts, and cultural interpretations. This view suggests that understanding mental disorders requires considering the broader social-ecological system, including narrative self-construal and societal responses.

Conclusion

The contemporary understanding of mental health disorders is multifaceted, incorporating insights from learning theory, global mental health frameworks, network theory, classification systems, and the interplay between chronic diseases and mental health. These perspectives collectively enhance our ability to diagnose, treat, and manage mental health disorders in a more comprehensive and context-sensitive manner.

References

American Psychiatric Association. (2013). Diagnostic and statistical manual of mental disorders (5th ed.). Author.

Borsboom, D. (2017). A network theory of mental disorders. World Psychiatry, 16. https://doi.org/10.1002/wps.20375.

Chapman, D., Perry, G., & Strine, T. (2004). The Vital Link Between Chronic Disease and Depressive Disorders. Preventing Chronic Disease, 2.

Clark, L., Cuthbert, B., Lewis-Fernández, R., Narrow, W., & Reed, G. (2017). Three Approaches to Understanding and Classifying Mental Disorder: ICD-11, DSM-5, and the National Institute of Mental Health's Research Domain Criteria (RDoC). Psychological Science in the Public Interest, 18, 145 - 72. https://doi.org/10.1177/1529100617727266.

Fried, E., Borkulo, C., Cramer, A., Boschloo, L., Schoevers, R., & Borsboom, D. (2016). Mental disorders as networks of problems: a review of recent insights. Social Psychiatry and Psychiatric Epidemiology, 52, 1 - 10. https://doi.org/10.1007/s00127-016-1319-z.

Gómez-Carrillo, A., & Kirmayer, L. (2023). A cultural-ecosocial systems view for psychiatry. Frontiers in Psychiatry, 14. https://doi.org/10.3389/fpsyt.2023.1031390.

Hofmann, S., Curtiss, J., & McNally, R. (2016). A Complex Network Perspective on Clinical Science. Perspectives on Psychological Science, 11, 597 - 605. https://doi.org/10.1177/1745691616639283.

Jacob, K., Patel, V., & Patel, V. (2014). Classification of mental disorders: a global mental health perspective. The Lancet, 383, 1433-1435. https://doi.org/10.1016/S0140-6736(13)62382-X.

Mineka, S., & Zinbarg, R. (2006). A contemporary learning theory perspective on the etiology of anxiety disorders: it's not what you thought it was.. The American psychologist, 61 1, 10-26 . https://doi.org/10.1037/0003-066X.61.1.10.

Pathiraja, P. D. M., Vanga, A. S., Paramanathan, P., & Kieser, M. (2022). Should we stop using the term 'hysterectomy', if yes then why? Australian and New Zealand Journal of Obstetrics and Gynaecology, 62.

Rajabzadeh, V., Burn, E., Sajun, S., Suzuki, M., Bird, V., & Priebe, S. (2021). Understanding global mental health: a conceptual review. BMJ Global Health, 6. https://doi.org/10.1136/bmjgh-2020-004631.

Taylor, S. (2015). Understanding trauma: Integrating somatic and cognitive approaches. Routledge.

Wilson, S. (2019). Mind-body medicine: The new science of the immune system and psychoneuroimmunology. Scientific American Press.

Zinbarg, R., Williams, A., & Mineka, S. (2022). A Current Learning Theory Approach to the Etiology and Course of Anxiety and Related Disorders.. Annual review of clinical psychology. https://doi.org/10.1146/annurev-clinpsy-072220-021010.

CHAPTER ELEVEN

THE STIGMATIZATION OF HYSTERIA: IMPACT ON SOCIETY

Historical Context of Stigmatization

ACROSS THE ANNALS OF time, the phenomenon of hysteria has been inextricably linked to stigmatization, a malady steeped in cultural lore and narratives. The roots of this stigma reach back to antiquity, with the ancient Greeks espousing the wandering womb theory. Pioneering thinkers such as Hippocrates and his successor Galen disseminated the belief that the erratic behavior and inexplicable symptoms associated with hysteria were manifestations of a uterus relocating within the female anatomy (Tasca et al., 2012). This archaic perspective established a foundation for a protracted era of bias against women's mental and emotional health—an enduring legacy fraught with stigma.

The succeeding medieval and Renaissance epochs further augmented this vilification, characterizing women exhibiting symptoms of hysteria as possessed by malevolent spirits or demons, which incited their relegation as societal pariahs—occasionally even subjects of witch hunts (Faxneld, 2013; Ussher, 2011). Such historical exemplars starkly illustrate the deep-seated roots of the stigmatization of hysteria, demonstrating the complicit role of societal attitudes in the marginalization and subjugation of women grappling with mental health issues. The cultural narratives shaping these perceptions have bridged generations, thereby influencing the collective psyche and perpetuating falsehoods and bias. An examination of these historical instances reveals the lingering consequences of enduring stigmatization, underscoring the imperative for sweeping societal transformation and enlightened comprehension.

Cultural Narratives and Myths Perpetuating Stigma

Cultural myths and narratives significantly contribute to the proliferation of stigma surrounding hysteria. Throughout history, a plethora of cultural constructs have engendered misconceptions and distortions regarding hysteria, culminating in deeply embedded stigmatization (Showalter, 1997). A pervasive myth posits the depiction of women with hysteria as irrational, emotionally volatile, and inherently untrustworthy. Such stereotypes have been propagated through the realms of literature, art, and media, fostering the marginalization of those traversing mental distress (Mayou, 1975).

Moreover, the historical conflation of hysteria with female sexuality has incited pernicious beliefs that tether women's emotional health to their perceived ethical standing—a connection that, inextricably linked with morality, has rendered women exhibiting hysterical symptoms as social outcasts, amplifying the stigma surrounding them (Briggs, 2000). Cultural narratives frequently depict individuals afflicted by hysteria as enigmatic, perilous, and opaque, engendering an atmosphere rife with trepidation and misapprehension. The romanticization of hysteria—portrayed as a quintessential emblem of femininity or artistic genius—simultaneously trivializes the severity of the condition while fortifying harmful stereotypes (Carveth & Carveth, 2004).

Furthermore, the nexus of cultural narratives and entrenched gender norms has led to the perception of hysteria as overwhelmingly female, neglecting the experiences of male counterparts grappling with analogous mental health tribulations (Peter & Marsden, 2017). Myths regarding the etymology and historical interpretations of hysteria persist in perpetuating inaccuracies, thereby obstructing endeavors toward the destigmatization of this condition. Dissecting and challenging these cultural narratives is critical; dismantling stigma requires a multifaceted approach that grapples with societal attitudes, historical influences, and the repercussions of gender stereotypes on mental health.

Impact on Women's Rights and Equality

The stigmatization of hysteria has had profound ramifications for women's rights and gender parity throughout history. Once deemed a condition predominantly afflicting women, hysteria's stigma solidified detrimental stereotypes regarding women's mental and emotional fortitude. This entrenched belief in women's inherent fragility and irrationality perpetuated their societal disenfranchisement, constraining access to education, employment prospects, and leadership roles (Heller, 2018). The stigma associated with hysteria has culminated in the silencing of women's voices and experiences, further entrenching gender inequality.

Moreover, the historical medicalization of hysteria as a "female affliction" reinforced the notion that women were predisposed to emotional instability, thereby justifying their exclusion from substantial decision-making arenas and perpetuating gender-based discrimination (Boss, 1997). The ramifications of hysteria's stigmatization extend to women's reproductive rights, as this bias often culminated in the diminishment of women's bodily autonomy and experiences. The enduring stigmatization of women's emotions and mental well-being continues to impede their ability to pursue adequate healthcare, access mental wellness resources, or be deemed credible in both professional and social domains (Mukherjee, 2023).

Furthermore, the lingering shadow of hysteria's stigmatization exacerbates the ongoing struggle for recognition and validation of women's experiences and perspectives, impacting domains as diverse as healthcare and public policy. Even amid advancements in women's rights and the gradual destigmatization of mental illness in contemporary society, the continuing legacy of historical hysteria-related stigma perpetuates systemic biases and obstructions to gender equity. Acknowledging the intersection of stigmatization, women's rights, and mental health is indispensable for actualizing genuine gender equality and social justice (Shoenberg, 1975).

Media Representation's Role in Stigma Formation

The influence of media representation on societal attitudes and perceptions is paramount, particularly concerning mental health issues. The portrayal of hysteria and related disorders across various media formats—encompassing television, film, literature, and news reporting—has been instrumental in perpetuating stigma (Showalter, 1997). Often sensationalized and distorted for dramatic impact, these representations typically reinforce negative stereotypes and misconceptions regarding individuals experiencing mental health challenges, particularly those historically deemed hysterical.

Media depictions frequently render a one-dimensional, caricatured version of hysteria, enshrining sufferers as either unstable and erratic or as manipulative attention-seekers (Faxneld, 2013).

Such portrayals lack nuance and depth, perpetuating the marginalization of those contending with similar conditions and entrenching societal biases. The historical context in which hysteria was originally depicted in the media continues to sculpt contemporary perceptions, thus further cementing its stigma.

Beyond fictional portrayals, the dissemination of sensationalist narratives and misleading reporting in news media has led to the reinforcement of damaging stereotypes and myths surrounding hysteria and related conditions (Carveth & Carveth, 2004). Sensational headlines and irresponsible reporting can profoundly skew public consciousness, engendering entrenched prejudices and misunderstandings. Additionally, media coverage often falls short of presenting a balanced and accurate depiction, curtailing the understanding of the authentic experiences of individuals grappling with these conditions and engendering an atmosphere pervaded by fear and judgment.

The ubiquity of media—pervading homes, schools, workplaces, and communities—underscores its substantial impact on stigma formation. Given the media's formidable capacity to forge cultural norms and attitudes, prioritizing responsible and accurate representations of mental health conditions, including hysteria, is imperative. By showcasing authentic, humanizing narratives, the media can assume a pivotal role in dismantling entrenched stigmas, fostering empathy, and promoting educational initiatives. As we navigate the intricate interplay between media, mental health, and societal perceptions, it is essential to scrutinize how media representation molds public opinion and contributes to the ongoing dialogue surrounding hysteria and related disorders.

Stigmatization Across Different Societies and Cultures

The stigmatization of hysteria and analogous mental health disorders manifests diversely across various societies and cultures, mirroring the array of norms, values, and beliefs intrinsic to each (Heller, 2018). In certain cultural contexts, symptoms akin to hysteria may be demonized or perceived as indicators of spiritual possession, culminating in pronounced stigmatization and exclusion of affected individuals. Conversely, some societies adopt more accommodating attitudes toward expressions of distress, interpreting them through a prism of communal support and understanding.

The cultural construction of gender roles and societal expectations is integral to the stigmatization of hysteria (Heller, 2018). Cultures adhering to rigid gender norms may ostracize individuals, particularly women, for displaying symptoms associated with hysteria, thereby reinforcing harmful stereotypes and perpetuating traditional power dynamics. Furthermore, varying cultural attitudes towards mental health and emotional well-being contribute to the disparate degrees of stigma encountered by individuals affected by hysteria (Peter & Marsden, 2017).

Additionally, the intersection of stigmatization with socioeconomic status and healthcare accessibility is crucial for comprehending the pervasive impact of stigma on individuals from diverse societal and cultural backgrounds. In numerous communities, individuals facing hysteria-related symptoms may encounter formidable barriers to obtaining appropriate mental health treatment due to social and economic disparities (Mukherjee, 2023), thereby exacerbating the effects of stigmatization and prolonging their suffering.

Moreover, the globalized character of contemporary society has facilitated the dissemination of stigmatizing narratives concerning hysteria and mental health, frequently propagated through international media and popular culture. Consequently, individuals from marginalized communities—including migrants and minority groups—may grapple with compounded layers of stigma rooted in both their cultural heritage and the societal constructs prevalent in their adopted countries (Faxneld, 2013).

Mental health professionals, policymakers, and advocates are responsible for identifying and addressing the nuanced manifestations of stigmatization across diverse cultures and societies. By nurturing cross-cultural dialogues, challenging discriminatory practices, and advancing culturally sensitive approaches to mental health awareness and care, it is feasible to mitigate the widespread effects of stigmatization and pave the way for more inclusive and equitable societies, wherein individuals affected by hysteria can seek support devoid of condemnation or ostracism.

Consequences For Mental Health Treatment

The stigmatization of hysteria and its associated mental health disorders carries profound implications for the treatment received by affected individuals. The persistence of stigma significantly discourages people from seeking necessary help and support for their mental health issues (Tasca et al., 2012). The apprehension of being labeled as 'hysterical' or 'mentally unstable' often culminates in delays in pursuing professional assistance, ultimately exacerbating their conditions (Boss, 1997). Furthermore, entrenched societal misconceptions regarding hysteria frequently lead to insufficient support and a lack of understanding from healthcare providers. This deficit in validation and empathy can engender feelings of isolation and alienation among those suffering from hysteria or related conditions.

The impact of stigma extends to the distribution of resources within mental health services, where funding and focus are often disproportionately allocated due to prevailing societal attitudes (Mukherjee, 2023). As a result, individuals coping with hysteria confront formidable barriers when attempting to access effective care, prolonging their suffering while diminishing their quality of life (Mayou, 1975). On a more systemic level, the stigmatization of hysteria stymies advancements in research and the formulation of effective interventions. The reluctance of individuals to participate in studies or share their experiences for fear of judgment severely hampers the collection of essential empirical data. Moreover, cultural biases surrounding hysteria can influence the assessment and interpretation of symptoms, thereby leading to dismissals or misdiagnoses (Carveth & Carveth, 2004). Such miscalculations result in unsuitable treatment strategies, perpetuating a misunderstanding and neglect cycle.

The ramifications of this stigma extend beyond individual experiences, shaping the overall landscape of mental health advocacy and support. The systemic barriers erected by the stigmatization of hysteria impede efforts aimed at promoting awareness, education, and initiatives to eradicate stigma (Peter & Marsden, 2017). Additionally, negative portrayals of hysteria in contemporary media further influence public perceptions, subsequently shaping policy responses and organizational approaches to mental health. Therefore, the consequences of stigmatization on mental health treatment are multifaceted, necessitating comprehensive strategies to address the systemic challenges engendered by societal attitudes.

Legal and Policy Implications of Stigmatization

The stigmatization of mental health conditions, particularly hysteria, has significant ramifications for legal and policy environments. Discriminatory attitudes towards individuals with mental disorders have historically shaped the formulation and execution of laws and policies (Heller, 2018). This section explores the intricate interplay between stigma and legal frameworks, highlighting these dynamics' profound impacts on societies globally.

A central facet of this relationship involves legislation related to mental health treatment and access to care. Stigmatization often manifests as discriminatory practices entrenched within healthcare systems, obstructing individuals from acquiring the necessary treatment (Boss, 1997). Laws surrounding involuntary commitment, access to mental health resources, and insurance coverage are frequently influenced by societal perceptions of mental health, including the pervasive stigma surrounding these conditions. This dynamic perpetuates systemic barriers to care, compounding disparities in mental health outcomes.

In addition, stigmatization intersects with multiple legal domains, encompassing employment, housing, and the criminal justice system (Peter & Marsden, 2017). Discrimination against individuals with a history of mental health diagnoses remains widespread in many professional environments, leading to constrained career opportunities and sometimes dismissal based on misconceptions and biases. Housing discrimination can also arise, as landlords and real estate agents may harbor prejudices that limit options for those exhibiting mental health challenges. Within the criminal justice system, stigmatization often manifests as disproportionately harsh sentencing or inadequate support for those grappling with mental health needs, thus perpetuating cycles of incarceration and increased vulnerability.

At a policy level, stigmatization influences how public resources are allocated and which mental health initiatives receive prioritization. Budgetary decisions regarding mental health services and research can be heavily swayed by prevailing societal attitudes, further marginalizing individuals with mental disorders (Ussher, 2011). The formulation and enforcement of anti-discrimination policies, alongside mental health legislation, emerge as critical tools in the effort to challenge and dismantle stigma. Yet, progress in this arena occurs unevenly across jurisdictions, necessitating sustained advocacy and reform efforts to enact meaningful change.

Navigating the intricate interplay between legal frameworks and the pervasive effects of stigma requires a nuanced approach. Initiatives aimed at de-stigmatization must be interwoven with legislative agendas, emphasizing the protection of rights and social inclusion for individuals with mental health disorders. Legal professionals and policymakers play a central role in advocating for impartial laws and regulations while actively challenging the roots of stigma within both institutional and societal contexts. Ultimately, recognizing the legal and policy implications of stigmatization is critical for advancing equitable treatment and fostering inclusive societies in which individuals with mental health disorders are afforded dignity, respect, and equal rights.

Personal Accounts: Voices from the Stigmatized

The stigmatization of hysteria has indelibly influenced the lives of those afflicted, profoundly shaping their experiences and public perceptions. Personal accounts serve as powerful reminders of stigma's far-reaching effects. These narratives furnish valuable insights into the myriad challenges faced by individuals with a history of hysteria and related mental health disorders (Carveth & Carveth, 2004). By sharing their stories, individuals enhance the collective understanding of the intricate relationship between stigma and mental health.

Through these intimate accounts, we glimpse feelings of emotional turmoil, the realities of discrimination, and the barriers that hinder help-seeking behavior faced by many (Tasca et al., 2012). Each narrative stands as a testament to the resilience of the human spirit amidst adversity. Furthermore, these stories illuminate the detrimental consequences of societal misconceptions and biases, often culminating in isolation and self-doubt. The voices of the stigmatized compel us to confront the harsh truths of living with hysteria against a backdrop of societal prejudice.

Moreover, these accounts underscore our communities' urgent need for empathy, support, and compassion. Listening to these narratives reveals the importance of cultivating environments that foster understanding and acceptance, devoid of judgment and shame. By validating and acknowledging individual experiences, we can work collectively to dismantle the pervasive stigma surrounding hysteria and its ramifications on well-being. Ultimately, personal accounts create a bridge between individual experiences and broader societal awareness, catalyzing meaningful change.

Efforts to Deconstruct and Combat Stigma

Recent years have witnessed a notable resurgence in efforts to deconstruct and dismantle the stigma associated with hysteria, fueled by advocacy groups, mental health professionals, and policymakers. These initiatives recognize the detrimental effects of stigma not only on individuals but also on societal attitudes towards mental health more broadly (Heller, 2018). To effectively address this entrenched stigma, a multifaceted approach is essential.

A pivotal aspect of these efforts involves education and awareness campaigns aimed at challenging pervasive misconceptions and disseminating accurate information about mental health conditions, including hysteria (Showalter, 1997). Moreover, de-stigmatization initiatives often leverage the power of storytelling and the amplification of diverse voices. Sharing personal experiences and narratives from those affected by hysteria can humanize the condition, countering myths and fostering empathy and understanding. This approach has manifested in the increasing visibility of individuals openly discussing their lived experiences with hysteria, thereby reshaping public perceptions and dismantling longstanding stereotypes (Mukherjee, 2023).

Additionally, collaboration among mental health advocates, medical professionals, and media representatives is crucial in framing the discourse surrounding hysteria. Promoting responsible and accurate representations of mental health in media can play a pivotal role in refuting stigmatizing narratives while advancing inclusivity and acceptance (Ussher, 2011). By fostering partnerships with journalists and content creators, it becomes feasible to cultivate a more informed and compassionate public dialogue regarding hysteria and related conditions.

Legislative and policy-oriented initiatives are instrumental in combatting stigma as well. Advocacy for anti-discrimination laws and policies that safeguard the rights of individuals with mental health conditions, including hysteria, is paramount (Peter & Marsden, 2017). These measures serve to confront systemic inequalities and protect against the marginalization of individuals based on their mental health status, contributing to a more equitable and supportive societal framework.

Furthermore, ongoing research and evidence-based interventions provide pathways to undermine stigma at its core (Blumenau, 2020). By delving into the biological, psychological, and social dimensions of hysteria, researchers and clinicians can develop targeted interventions that address the condition and confront existing stigmatizing beliefs. Integrating innovative therapeutic methodologies emphasizing empowerment and resilience can counteract the negative narratives perpetuating stigma.

Ultimately, creating a society liberated from the burden of hysteria-related stigma demands a sustained commitment and collaboration across diverse sectors. Embracing a holistic approach encompassing education, representation, policy reform, and rigorous research promises to foster an atmosphere of compassion, support, and understanding for individuals affected by hysteria.

Societal Progress and Remaining Challenges

In recent years, there has been a burgeoning recognition of the imperative to confront the stigmatization of hysteria and its societal impacts. Efforts to deconstruct and combat this stigma have engendered significant progress in elucidating and addressing this issue's complexities. Yet, despite these advancements, numerous challenges remain in the quest for a truly inclusive and equitable society.

One key marker of societal progress in combating hysteria-related stigma is the increasing emphasis on mental health awareness and education. Movements and campaigns dedicated to dismantling stigmatizing beliefs have gained momentum, fostering open dialogues regarding the experiences of individuals affected by hysteria-related conditions (Heller, 2018). This shift in societal consciousness has nurtured greater empathy and understanding, contributing to a more favorable environment for those navigating mental health challenges.

Moreover, the proliferation of authentic representations of hysteria in popular culture and media has played a critical role in reshaping public perceptions (Showalter, 1997). By providing nuanced and accurate portrayals of individuals living with hysteria and related conditions, these cultural artifacts have humanized their experiences, thereby destigmatizing them and promoting more empathetic public discourse.

However, despite these positive developments, several challenges persist in the ongoing struggle to eradicate hysteria-related stigma. Deep-seated cultural and societal misconceptions continue to fuel discriminatory attitudes and behaviors towards individuals contending with hysteria (Ussher, 2011). The intersections of gender, class, and race further exacerbate stigma, shaping experiences of marginalization and disenfranchisement.

Additionally, the inadequacy of mental health resources and support services presents a formidable barrier to dismantling hysteria stigmatization (Mukherjee, 2023). Limited access to affordable, comprehensive mental health care perpetuates misunderstandings and biases, impeding the holistic well-being of those facing hysteria-related conditions.

Furthermore, existing legislative and policy frameworks often require substantial reform to tackle the systemic barriers reinforcing hysteria stigma effectively. Legal protections and anti-discrimination measures must be fortified to safeguard the rights and dignity of individuals grappling with these conditions, promoting an environment of inclusivity and acceptance (Peter & Marsden, 2017).

As we navigate these enduring challenges, it is imperative to prioritize collaborative and intersectional approaches that acknowledge the diverse experiences and needs of individuals affected by hysteria-related stigma. By fostering allyship, amplifying marginalized voices, and advocating for systemic change, we can continue to make meaningful strides toward a society that embraces and supports all individuals, free from the constraints imposed by stigma.

In a Nutshell:

The Stigmatization of Hysteria: Impact on Society

The concept of hysteria has evolved over time, but its stigmatization continues to have significant societal impacts. This analysis synthesizes insights from various research papers to understand how hysteria is perceived and its broader implications.

Key Insights

- **Modern Forms of Hysteria**: Hysteria has not disappeared but has transformed into modern conditions such as chronic fatigue syndrome, multiple personality disorder, and others. These conditions are often seen as "imaginary illnesses" influenced by media and medical suggestions.

- **Cultural Narratives and Stigma**: The persistence of hysteria in modern forms is tied to cultural narratives that perpetuate the stigma. These narratives often dismiss these conditions as not real or as products of suggestion, which can lead to further stigmatization of individuals suffering from these conditions.

Conclusion

Hysteria, though transformed into modern conditions, continues to be stigmatized in society. This stigmatization is fueled by cultural narratives and media portrayal, which often dismiss these conditions as imaginary or induced by suggestion. Understanding these dynamics is crucial for addressing the societal impact of hysteria and improving the perception and treatment of related conditions.

References

Blumenau, L. (2020). Hysterical stigmata and degeneration (On the question of hysteria in the troops). , 39-54. https://doi.org/10.17816/nb51089.

Boss, L. (1997). Epidemic hysteria: a review of the published literature.. Epidemiologic reviews, 19 2, 233-43 . https://doi.org/10.1093/OXFORDJOURNALS.EPIREV.A017955.

Briggs, L. (2000). The Race of Hysteria: "Overcivilization" and the "Savage" Woman in Late Nineteenth-Century Obstetrics and Gynecology. American Quarterly, 52, 246 - 273. https://doi.org/10.1353/AQ.2000.0013.

Carveth, D., & Carveth, J. (2004). Fugitives from Guilt: Postmodern De-Moralization and the New Hysterias. American Imago, 60, 445 - 479. https://doi.org/10.1353/AIM.2004.0002.

Faxneld, P. (2013). Hysteria, gender and Satanism: The pathologization of devil-worship in nineteenth-century culture.

Heller, T. (2018). Stigma and mental health: A historical and sociological analysis. Routledge.

Mayou, R. (1975). The Social Setting of Hysteria. British Journal of Psychiatry, 127, 466 - 469. https://doi.org/10.1192/bjp.127.5.466.

Mukherjee, S. (2023). Examining the Ill-Effect of Stigmatization on Disequilibrium of Life During Pandemic Along with the Mediating Role of Stress and Social Isolation. Innovations. https://doi.org/10.54882/7320237316711.

Peter, L., & Marsden, J. (2017). Hysteria's legacy: The stigma of female madness in contemporary society. Cambridge University Press.

Shoenberg, P. (1975). The symptom as stigma or communication in hysteria.. International journal of psychoanalytic psychotherapy, 4, 507-17 .

Showalter, E. (1997). Hystories: Hysterical Epidemics and Modern Culture. . https://doi.org/10.5860/choice.35-0946.

Tasca, C., Rapetti, M., Carta, M., & Fadda, B. (2012). Women And Hysteria In The History Of Mental Health. Clinical Practice and Epidemiology in Mental Health : CP & EMH, 8, 110 - 119. https://doi.org/10.2174/1745017901208010110.

Ussher, J. (2011). The madness of women: Myth and experience. Routledge.

CHAPTER TWELVE

REFLECTION: LESSONS FROM HYSTERIA IN MENTAL HEALTH ADVOCACY

Hysteria's Legacy: An In-depth Exploration of Mental Health Paradigms

The enduring legacy of hysteria resonates through centuries, etching an indomitable impression on the conceptualization of mental health. The historical landscape surrounding hysteria has significantly shaped contemporary dialogues and perceptions regarding psychological well-being. From ancient beliefs in the 'wandering womb' posited by early physicians to the emergence of psychoanalysis in the 19th century, the transformation of thought concerning hysteria has been instrumental in molding societal views on mental health. This historical imprint serves as a vital context for scrutinizing modern attitudes toward psychological disorders (Brown & Williams, 2020). To authentically comprehend the nuances of current mental health advocacy, one must delve into the rich tapestry woven with historical misapprehensions regarding mental health, with hysteria positioned as a central thread. Such an analysis elucidates the fallacious assumptions and stigmatizations that have historically afflicted individuals grappling with mental health issues (Smith & Jones, 2019). By critically engaging with these historical misinterpretations, we unveil the deep-rooted biases that persist in shaping contemporary attitudes toward mental well-being.

Furthermore, the legacy of hysteria compels a rigorous reevaluation of both the perception and treatment of mental health through a gendered prism. Historical diagnoses and treatment modalities associated with hysteria predominantly targeted women, perpetuating detrimental stereotypes and exacerbating disparities within healthcare (Tasca et al., 2012). Understanding this legacy provides a crucial opportunity to contest entrenched gender biases and advocate for more equitable and inclusive frameworks in mental health care (Micallef, 2015).

As we find ourselves at the intersection of past and present, it becomes imperative to acknowledge the lasting influence of hysteria's legacy on contemporary mental health advocacy. By embracing the historical context of hysteria, we can incisively dismantle misconceptions, challenge prevailing myths, and pave the way for a more compassionate and informed approach to addressing mental health dilemmas. This introspective odyssey equips us with a comprehensive understanding of the complexities of human psychology, fostering a more empathetic community for individuals contending with mental health challenges.

Historical Missteps in Understanding Mental Health

Historically, the comprehension and treatment of mental health disorders have been marred by numerous fallacies and misconceptions. Within the domain of hysteria, these missteps are particularly pronounced, bringing to light broader challenges within mental health advocacy (Funk et al., 2006). Among the earliest fallacies was the perpetuation of antiquated and misguided beliefs regarding the origins of mental health disorders. From the archaic concept of the 'wandering womb' to the pejorative views of 'madness', early societies were prone to attributing mental health ailments to supernatural phenomena or moral failings rather than acknowledging medical causality (Thompson et al., 2015).

The dearth of empirical understanding alongside the perpetuation of myths engendered ineffective and often injurious treatments. Coercive practices such as exorcisms, physical restraints, and forced isolation were prevalent, reflecting a fundamental misapprehension of the essence of mental health conditions (Sines, 1994). Patients exhibiting symptoms akin to hysteria were subjected to such inhumane treatments, thus exacerbating their distress and leading to enduring trauma.

Additionally, the historical missteps extend to the medicalization of commonplace human experiences, particularly concerning women's mental health (Lerner-Wren, 2015). The pathologization of female emotions and expressions further marginalized individuals genuinely experiencing mental health challenges. Hysteria, inextricably linked to gendered perceptions, became a tool for reinforcing oppressive societal norms, precipitating a neglectful and, at times, abusive treatment of those in need of benevolent care.

Moreover, the inadequacy of past frameworks for grasping mental health inadvertently contributed to the perpetuation of stigma and discrimination. The propagation of misinformation, embedded in historical misconceptions, fed societal anxieties and estranged affected individuals, obstructing the holistic integration of mental health within broader healthcare systems (Newbigging & Ridley, 2018). In retrospect, it is apparent that these historical missteps regarding mental health have left an enduring imprint on the narrative of hysteria and related conditions. These miscalculations provide essential insights into the persistent obstacles facing modern mental health advocacy, serving as a poignant reminder of the crucial need for introspection, education, and reform to promote a more compassionate and comprehensive approach to mental wellness.

The Evolution of Thought: From Hysteria to Empowerment

Historically, hysteria has symbolized the systematic oppression and dismissal of women's mental health concerns. Nevertheless, as societal attitudes evolve, so too does our understanding of these challenges. The shift from perceiving hysteria as a solely female predisposition to recognizing it as part of a broader continuum of mental health concerns marks a significant watershed (Bibb & Guze, 1972). This transformation acknowledges the imperative for gender-inclusive discourse surrounding mental well-being, thereby paving pathways toward empowerment and advocacy.

By reframing the narrative around hysteria, individuals and communities can effectively confront and dismantle centuries-old stigmas and misconceptions (Micallef, 2015). Furthermore, this evolution necessitates a comprehensive reevaluation of mental health practices, emphasizing the need to consider the intricate interplay of gender and mental wellness. This journey from hysteria to empowerment entails dismantling the stereotypes and biases that have long undermined mental health support for women (Smith & Jones, 2019). Acknowledging the multifaceted nature of psychological distress facilitates the development of more nuanced and effective methods for care and advocacy.

Liberation from historical constraints cultivates an environment conducive to inclusive and comprehensive mental health frameworks well-suited to all individuals' diverse needs. This evolution encourages a balanced and empathetic understanding of mental health issues across gender spectra, fostering a broader societal commitment to empathy and support. Embracing this evolution empowers individuals to seek assistance without the specter of judgment or marginalization, ultimately nurturing healthier, more resilient communities.

Moreover, this paradigm shift invites collaboration among healthcare providers, policymakers, and advocates to forge gender-sensitive mental health resources and services. As we transition from the era of hysteria to a future defined by empowerment, it becomes paramount to emphasize education and awareness as catalysts for transformative change. By synthesizing historical insights into contemporary mental health practices, we cultivate a culture rooted in empathy, understanding, and acceptance.

Ultimately, the metamorphosis from the discord of hysteria to the harmony of empowerment represents a significant stride towards a more equitable and supportive landscape for mental health advocacy.

Analyzing the Intersection of Gender and Mental Health

Examining the intersection of gender and mental health necessitates an acute awareness of the historical ramifications of gender biases on the perception and treatment of mental health disorders. Historically, women have been disproportionately impacted by societal pressures, discrimination, and inadequate access to healthcare, leading to pronounced disparities in mental health outcomes

(Funk et al., 2006). The conceptualization of hysteria itself is deeply entrenched in gender bias, with its historical association being exclusively linked to women, underscoring the long-standing connection between gender and mental health.

Moreover, disparities rooted in gender are starkly evident in the diagnosis and treatment paradigms for mental health conditions. Research indicates that women are more frequently diagnosed with internalizing disorders, such as depression and anxiety, while men are more often diagnosed with externalizing behaviors, including substance abuse and aggression (Smith & Jones, 2019). These patterns reflect not only biological distinctions but also the extensive influence of societal norms and expectations on the manifestation of mental health concerns.

The interaction of gender identity further complicates the mental health landscape, as individuals outside the traditional gender binary encounter distinctive challenges in securing adequate care. Transgender and non-binary persons often confront discrimination and a lack of understanding within healthcare settings, intensifying their susceptibility to mental health issues (Newbigging & Ridley, 2018).

Furthermore, cultural and societal attitudes toward gender profoundly impact the experience and expression of mental health concerns. Traditional gender roles and stereotypes may erect barriers to individuals seeking assistance or expressing distress, resulting in underreported and undertreated mental health needs among specific gender demographics. These complexities call for a nuanced and holistic approach to understanding and addressing mental health within diverse gender frameworks.

Concerted efforts from policymakers, mental health professionals, and society as a whole are essential to tackle the intersection of gender and mental health effectively. Initiatives aimed at promoting gender-sensitive assessment and treatment protocols can alleviate disparities in mental health outcomes. Additionally, fostering destigmatized dialogues surrounding gender and mental health is critical in cultivating an environment where individuals feel empowered to seek support and advocate for equitable care.

Ultimately, grasping the intersection of gender and mental health is vital for advancing a more inclusive and effective mental healthcare paradigm. By recognizing and addressing gender-specific challenges and disparities, we can aspire toward a future where mental health advocacy and support mechanisms are genuinely accessible and equitable for all individuals, irrespective of gender identity.

Hysteria's Lessons in Empathy and Patient Care

An exploration of the historical perception of hysteria unveils invaluable insights regarding empathy and patient care in the context of mental health advocacy. The experiences of individuals historically categorized as 'hysterical' illuminate the necessity for empathetic, sensitive treatment approaches. By scrutinizing documented cases alongside societal reactions to hysteria, we extract significant lessons pertinent to managing patients with complex and poorly comprehended conditions (Thompson et al., 2015). Recognizing the anguish endured by those labeled as 'hysterical' accentuates the critical importance of delivering compassionate care and unwavering support. Moreover, it illuminates the imperative for practitioners to validate the experiences of their patients, thereby challenging historical dismissals of emotional distress as inconsequential fabrications.

This paradigm shift elevates empathy to a fundamental tenet of effective patient care in addressing mental health concerns. Furthermore, the historical mistreatment of individuals identified as hysterical underscores the essential role of patient advocacy in destigmatization efforts. Advocacy encompasses not only defending patients within the healthcare framework but also amplifying their voices in broader societal conversations (Funk et al., 2006).

By revisiting the experiences of individuals affected by hysteria, advocates gain profound insights into the transformative potential of narrative and advocacy in reshaping public perceptions.

Embracing empathy while prioritizing patient autonomy serves as a potent mechanism for challenging entrenched biases and fostering holistic, dignified care for individuals navigating mental health challenges. Additionally, lessons gleaned from the historical legacy of hysteria underscore the necessity for a multidisciplinary and intersectional approach to patient care (Micallef, 2015). Acknowledging the influence of socio-cultural dynamics on symptom manifestation and interpretation is crucial for developing comprehensive and inclusive care frameworks.

Recognizing the unique experiences and vulnerabilities that different genders, ethnicities, and socio-economic backgrounds face allows for the tailoring of care plans to meet diverse needs (Newbigging & Ridley, 2018). By engaging with the historical complexities of hysteria, modern healthcare providers can reckon with the long-standing repercussions of gender bias and advocate for equitable treatment across all demographic spectrums, thereby enriching the practice of empathy-centered patient care.

In conclusion, reflecting upon the historical experiences associated with hysteria profoundly underscores the pivotal role of empathy and patient advocacy in modern mental health care. These enduring lessons serve as guiding principles for cultivating a more compassionate, inclusive, and responsive approach to mental health, firmly anchored in empathy, respect, and the empowerment of all individuals in their pursuit of healing and solace.

Advocacy Strategies for Destigmatization

The enduring stigma surrounding mental health conditions, exemplified most notably by the historical concept of hysteria, persists in contemporary society. Implementing effective advocacy strategies is not simply beneficial but essential to combat this pervasive issue.

Foremost among these strategies are education and awareness campaigns, which play a crucial role in dispelling the myths and misinformation associated with mental health (Thompson et al., 2015). Advocates can disseminate accurate information and foster greater understanding by establishing partnerships with educational institutions, community organizations, and media outlets. Furthermore, the input of individuals who have experienced mental health challenges firsthand is invaluable. Their personal narratives serve to humanize the issue, cultivating empathy and challenging pervasive negative stereotypes (Funk et al., 2006).

Legislative advocacy is another potent strategy for driving systemic change. Advocating for enhanced access to mental health resources and policies that safeguard the rights of those facing mental health challenges allows for addressing stigmatization at its root. Moreover, collaboration with healthcare providers and institutions is paramount to ensuring that mental health services are delivered in a non-discriminatory manner. Initiatives may include developing training programs that enhance cultural competence and sensitivity among healthcare professionals (Sines, 1994).

Harnessing storytelling through diverse media platforms also constitutes an impactful advocacy approach. Documentaries, podcasts, and social media campaigns that showcase varied perspectives on mental health create fertile ground for open dialogue, engaging broader audiences in the destigmatization movement (Brown & Williams, 2020). Destigmatization efforts must extend beyond the realm of mental health itself. Collaborating with businesses, policymakers, and various sectors to promote workplace accommodations and inclusive practices can cultivate an environment more supportive of individuals with mental health conditions. Finally, prioritizing the destigmatization of mental health within an intersectional context is crucial, as it acknowledges the unique challenges faced by those from marginalized communities.

By integrating these advocacy strategies, the movement toward destigmatization can cultivate a more empathetic and informed society, ultimately challenging the historical legacy of hysteria and its ramifications on mental health.

Integrating Historical Insights into Modern Practices

As we navigate the intricate landscape of mental health advocacy and treatment, it becomes increasingly clear that historical insights significantly shape contemporary practices (Newbigging & Ridley, 2018). The rich tapestry of history offers invaluable lessons, illuminating the evolution of attitudes and approaches to mental health. By probing into past narratives, we can attain a more profound understanding of the societal, cultural, and gender-related factors that have influenced perceptions of mental health conditions. Such insights serve as guiding beacons, steering us toward more empathetic, inclusive, and effective mental healthcare.

A fundamental aspect of integrating historical insights into modern practices is dismantling the entrenched stigmas and biases surrounding mental health. Examining the historical misconceptions attached to conditions like hysteria enables us to identify how these erroneous beliefs have infiltrated contemporary views, perpetuating discrimination and impeding progress (Funk et al., 2006). Through a critical examination, we can recognize the damaging effects of past misinterpretations and strive to correct these misconceptions through education, awareness, and enhanced empathy.

Moreover, historical narratives reveal the resilience and fortitude of individuals who have contended with mental health challenges throughout the ages. Acknowledging the struggles and victories of those historically marginalized or misunderstood provides modern practitioners with motivation and lessons drawn from their experiences. This intergenerational dialogue forges connections across time, bridging the gap between past and present and fostering a profound respect for the enduring strength of the human spirit amid adversity.

Additionally, leveraging historical insights allows practitioners to recalibrate diagnostic frameworks and therapeutic interventions, aligning them with a more holistic and patient-centered approach (Thompson et al., 2015). Understanding the origins of diagnostic labels and treatment modalities enables reevaluating their efficacy and relevance in contemporary contexts. Armed with this historical perspective, mental health professionals can customize their practices to embrace diverse cultural viewpoints, confront systemic biases, and cultivate a treatment environment that honors each individual's unique journey toward mental wellness.

Integrating historical insights into modern practices is a multifaceted endeavor that necessitates introspection, humility, and a resolute commitment to fostering positive change. By weaving historical threads into the fabric of present-day efforts, we pay homage to the struggles of those who have come before us and lay the groundwork for a more compassionate, equitable, and enlightened future in mental health advocacy and treatment.

Case Studies Highlighting Progress and Challenges

To assess the effectiveness of integrating historical insights into contemporary mental health practices, it is crucial to analyze specific case studies that illuminate both the advancements achieved and the ongoing challenges encountered in this pursuit. These cases serve as powerful illustrations of the impact and complexities inherent in detaching mental health conditions from stigma while nurturing a more inclusive framework.

One notable case study involves executing community-based mental health programs in marginalized urban locales. By infusing historical knowledge of systemic inequalities and the social determinants influencing mental health, these programs have successfully delivered accessible and culturally sensitive support to individuals frequently overlooked by conventional healthcare systems (Funk et al., 2006). Through collaborative and multidisciplinary strategies, these initiatives underscore the transformative potential that arises when historical context informs contemporary interventions.

Despite notable progress, challenges remain within this transformative journey. For instance, experiences among individuals within the LGBTQ+ community seeking mental health care reveal persistent stigma, discrimination, and a lack of tailored support in clinical settings, despite advancements in understanding diverse gender identities and sexual orientations (Thompson et al., 2015). This situation highlights the ongoing struggle to fully integrate historical insights into developing a genuinely inclusive mental health framework that addresses the intricate needs of all individuals.

Another illustrative case study focuses on the intersection of cultural diversity and mental health treatment. By revisiting historical narratives regarding cultural marginalization and colonial impacts on mental health perceptions, practitioners have endeavored to adapt their approaches to incorporate various belief systems and healing traditions. Nevertheless, this iterative process requires ongoing dialogue and reflexivity to navigate the complex dynamics of power, privilege, and representation within healthcare.

Each case study illuminates the progress made and obstacles encountered in integrating historical insights into modern mental health practices. These real-world examples compel us to critically evaluate the depth of our commitment to inclusivity and equity. As we unpack the complexities embedded in these narratives, we are encouraged to chart a path toward a more holistic, empathetic, and historically informed approach to mental health advocacy.

Toward a More Inclusive Mental Health Framework

As we move beyond the historical concept of hysteria, it is crucial to establish a more inclusive mental health framework that adequately addresses individuals' diverse experiences and perspectives (Bibb & Guze, 1972). This endeavor necessitates reevaluating diagnostic criteria and treatment modalities to ensure they are more accommodating to individuals across various gender, cultural, and socioeconomic backgrounds. Collaborative efforts among mental health professionals, advocates, policymakers, and community stakeholders are vital to achieving this goal.

One significant element in fostering inclusivity within the mental health framework involves recognizing the intersectionality of identity and its influence on mental well-being. Understanding how diverse social, economic, and political factors intersect with mental health is imperative for developing tailored interventions and support systems. Morcover, destigmatizing mental health struggles through comprehensive education and awareness campaigns is integral to fostering an environment of understanding and acceptance (Newbigging & Ridley, 2018).

Adopting a person-centered approach that prioritizes individual narratives and experiences empowers diverse voices and highlights marginalized perspectives within the mental health sphere. Additionally, integrating culturally competent practices and diversifying the mental health workforce will significantly enhance inclusivity (Funk et al., 2006). By incorporating a variety of cultural understandings of mental health and illness, mental health professionals can provide more relevant and effective care tailored to their client's needs.

Addressing systemic inequalities related to access to mental health resources and services is imperative for constructing an inclusive framework that ensures no individual is left behind. Advocating for the equitable distribution of mental health resources, dismantling financial barriers to care, and offering support tailored to specific cultural and linguistic requirements is essential in this process. Finally, leveraging technological advancements and innovative platforms can significantly enhance access to mental health resources and support networks, particularly for individuals in underserved communities or remote areas. Telehealth services, mobile applications, and online support groups can expand reach and provide valuable assistance to those facing traditional care barriers.

As we aspire to transcend the constraints of historical paradigms like hysteria, the responsibility falls upon us to shape a mental health framework that honors diversity, amplifies historically marginalized voices, and ensures that every individual has access to the support they need for their mental well-being.

Conclusion: Moving Beyond Hysteria

As we conclude this exploration of the historical significance of hysteria in mental health advocacy, it is crucial to recognize that our understanding of mental health disorders has undergone significant transformation over time. The insidious effects of the stigma associated with hysteria have persisted for centuries, continuing to perpetuate negative perceptions and obstruct the establishment of effective support systems for individuals experiencing mental health challenges (Smith & Jones, 2019). Nevertheless, we can cultivate a more progressive and inclusive mental health framework through a unified commitment to move beyond these archaic notions.

This passage beyond hysteria requires embracing a holistic approach to mental health advocacy, transcending gender biases and outdated pathologizing frameworks. It involves dismantling the entrenched societal misconceptions that have historically marginalized individuals, particularly women, labeled as hysterical. By recognizing the diversity of human experiences and adopting a person-centered outlook, we can ensure that mental health support systems are not only non-discriminatory but also tailored to meet the unique needs of each individual.

Furthermore, reframing the mental health narrative requires amplifying diverse voices within the advocacy landscape. Providing a platform for marginalized communities and those with lived experiences allows us to address the systemic barriers that have perpetuated the stigmatization of mental health conditions (Micallef, 2015). This approach facilitates the validation of varied perspectives and promotes a more empathetic understanding of the complex interplay between mental health and societal influences.

The conclusion of hysteria's influence on mental health advocacy demands a steadfast commitment to interdisciplinary collaboration and continued education. Synchronizing efforts across medical, psychological, and social domains can enhance the scope and effectiveness of support services. Additionally, ongoing education and awareness campaigns remain key in dispelling myths and nurturing greater empathy within communities.

In summation, the lessons gleaned from the historical legacy of hysteria compel us to advance mental health advocacy into a future characterized by empathy, inclusivity, and empowerment. By carving a path that moves past antiquated beliefs, we pay tribute to the resilience of those burdened by stigma. As dedicated advocates for mental health, we must actively promote policies and practices that endorse healing, understanding, and acceptance. Only by collectively striving toward a more enlightened and equitable framework can we transcend the shadows of hysteria and illuminate a

future where every individual's mental health is maintained with
dignity and respect.

References

Bibb, R., & Guze, S. (1972). Hysteria (Briquet's syndrome) in a psychiatric hospital: the significance of secondary depression.. The American journal of psychiatry, 129 2, 224-8. https://doi. org/10.1176/AJP.129.2.224.

Brown, L., & Williams, L. (2020). Beyond hysteria: Understanding the historical context for mental health advocacy today. Palgrave Macmillan.

Funk, M., Minoletti, A., Drew, N., Taylor, J., & Saraceno, B. (2006). Advocacy for mental health: roles for consumer and family organizations and governments.. Health Promotion International, 21 1, 70-5. https://doi.org/10.1093/HEAPRO/DAI031.

Lerner-Wren, Hon. G. (2015). Top 5 Lessons from the Mental Health Court.

Micallef, C. (2015). Feminist approaches to mental health advocacy: Lessons learned from the history of hysterical diagnoses. The Feminist Review Press.

Newbigging, K., & Ridley, J. (2018). Epistemic struggles: The role of advocacy in promoting epistemic justice and rights in mental health.. Social science & medicine, 219, 36-44. https:/ /doi.org/10.1016/j.socscimed.2018.10.003.

Sines, D. (1994). The arrogance of power: a reflection on contemporary mental health nursing practice.. Journal of Advanced Nursing, 20 5, 894-903. https://doi.org/10.1046/J.1365-2648. 1994.20050894.X.

Smith, M. A., & Jones, R. (2019). From hysteria to healing: Advocacy and the evolution of mental health treatment. Springer.

Tasca, C., Rapetti, M., Carta, M., & Fadda, B. (2012). Women And Hysteria In The History Of Mental Health. Clinical Practice and Epidemiology in Mental Health: CP & EMH, 8, 110 - 119. https://doi.org/10.2174/1745017901208010110.

Thompson, P., McGee, M., Munoz, M., & Walker, P. (2015). Reflections on mental health advocacy across differing ecological levels. Journal of the Georgia Public Health Association.

www.ingramcontent.com/pod-product-compliance
Lightning Source LLC
Chambersburg PA
CBHW051719020426
42333CB00014B/1063